GREAT FIRES
OF **LONDON**

This book is dedicated to all those who have worn the proud uniform of the London Fire Brigade and its predecessors, the Metropolitan Fire Brigade and the London Fire Engine Establishment, and to the present-day firefighters who protect the capital city and its population from the ravages of fire.

GREAT FIRES
OF LONDON

IMAGES OF THE LONDON FIRE BRIGADE
AT WORK SINCE 1833

NEIL WALLINGTON

SUTTON PUBLISHING

First published in 2001 by
Sutton Publishing Limited · Phoenix Mill
Thrupp · Stroud · Gloucestershire ·GL5 2BU

British Library Cataloguing in Publication Data
A catalogue record for this book is available from the British Library

ISBN 0 7509 2818 2

Typesetting and origination by
Sutton Publishing Limited.
Printed and bound in England by
J.H. Haynes & Co. Ltd, Sparkford.

CONTENTS

A fireman, to be successful, must enter buildings. He must get in below, above, on every side; from opposite houses, over back walls, over side walls, through panels of doors, through windows, through skylights, through holes cut by himself in gates, walls and the roof. He must know how to reach the attic from the basement by ladders placed on half-burned stairs, and the basement from the attic by a rope made fast on a chimney. His whole success depends on his getting in and remaining there, and he must always carry his appliances with him, as without them he is of no use.

Captain (Sir) Eyre Massey Shaw, Chief Fire Officer of the Metropolitan Fire Brigade 1866–91, from his book *A Complete Manual on the Organisation, Machinery, Discipline and General Working of the Fire Brigade of London* (1876)

The 1971 Governmental Inquiry into the work of the Fire Service chaired by Sir Charles Cunningham concluded that:

A fireman must have special qualities. He must have physical courage. On occasions he must voluntarily face extremities of danger which confront few other people in time of peace. It is the element of risk and the demand for courage which sets a fireman's job apart from others.

But bravery is not the only personal quality needed. A fireman must be able to work as part of a closely integrated team, the watch to which he belongs. He must also be prepared to obey orders without question, especially on the fireground. At the same time he must be able to show initiative when working on his own. All of these qualities may be needed in other occupations; but we know of none in which, together with courage in the face of danger, they are needed in combination to such a degree as in the fire service.

FOREWORD

**KENSINGTON PALACE,
LONDON, W.8.**

HRH Prince Michael of Kent.

The London Fire Brigade has a proud tradition of selfless service to the people of our capital city. Ever since its origins back in the nineteenth century the Brigade has set examples of courage, skill and sheer tenacity which few of us could ever hope to emulate.

I am delighted, therefore, to write the foreword to this pictorial record of the Brigade's illustrious history.

In recent years I have had the opportunity to visit the London Fire Brigade and have seen how the commitment of the firefighters matches their modesty in describing their individual and collective achievements.

It is appropriate that the prints and photographs selected for inclusion in this book have been chosen by a former London Fire Brigade officer. Clearly this is a specialised subject where personal experiences add an extra dimension to the story.

I wish the London Fire Brigade every continued success and am sure this book will serve as an enduring reminder of the debt we owe to the men and women of this remarkable organisation.

Michael

The sheer physical effort of firefighting is well caught in the expressions of these two London firemen in Kentish Town, 1966. They have just emerged from tackling a deep-seated basement fire in Proto oxygen breathing apparatus. The goggles have not long been pushed up and the mouthpieces removed, but the mental image is one of thick blinding smoke, intense heat, high humidity and constant danger.

PRELUDE

The photographs and prints selected for inclusion in this book provide more than simply a pictorial history of firefighting and rescue in London spanning three centuries. They reflect the demographic changes that have occurred in our capital city and the ways in which the London Fire Brigade has itself evolved to meet the ever-changing demands placed upon it.

Consider, for example, the fact that before the advent of the railways and the internal combustion engine most people, including firefighters (or firemen as they were known then), usually worked close to where they lived, and Greater London as we know it today was a collection of local and essentially self-contained communities.

Contrast that with the London of the new millennium where the resident population is swelled every day by hundreds of thousands of commuters and visitors and where so many streets and roads, particularly in the centre of the city, seem almost permanently in a state of gridlock.

The pattern of fires has changed too. Long gone are the teeming riverside wharves and warehouses wherein some of London's most notable and spectacular blazes occurred. No longer, thanks to the enactment and enforcement of legislation, do we have the disastrous fires in hotels and boarding houses that were almost a weekly occurrence in the 1960s and early '70s.

Chief Fire Officer Brian Robinson, CBE, OstJ, QFSM, FIFireE.

Tragically, people are still dying in fires in London – more often than not in circumstances where their personal status, perhaps elderly or very young, perhaps infirm or by being disadvantaged through lack of employment, makes them far more vulnerable to fire.

The London Fire Brigade is rightly proud of its history and the many incidents portrayed in this book are an epitaph to the professionalism, tenacity and, in some cases, raw courage of firefighters through the ages.

Ironically they could also be said to represent our failures for there is nothing more true than the old adage that 'the best fire never happened, it was prevented'. That might be correct to a point, and with the emphasis today on fire prevention and community fire safety the day may come when fires, especially those resulting in death or injury, will become so few and far between as to warrant considerably more attention from the news media than they usually attract today.

That is all for the future. What we have here and now is a vivid portrayal of the work of the London firefighter, of human frailty and tragedy, of pathos and drama. The images are very real, believe me, and Neil Wallington has put his many years' experience as a professional firefighter and officer to good effect to trace in visual form the great fires of London.

He is to be congratulated – not simply for pulling together a panorama of our past but for providing a stark and timely reminder of the awesome and destructive force that fire can be.

Brian Robinson, CBE, OstJ, QFSM, FIFireE,
(Commissioner for Fire and Emergency Planning, London Fire and
Emergency Planning Authority)

AUTHOR'S NOTE

It was during my early service in the London Fire Brigade while researching some material for my first book that I visited the Brigade's photographic archives for the first time. Right from that initial visit I was captivated by the superb visual images which were contained there; images not just of Victorian and Edwardian firemen at work, but of a much wider historical perspective on London, and how the capital city and its people have changed over the years.

Through subsequent visits I gradually came to explore the photographic collection and to uncover many dramatic fire scenes as well as the endlessly fascinating and wonderful set-piece poses with new equipment, a fire station or simply a spotless horse-drawn fire engine and its brass helmeted crew.

I have always felt that these evocative fire service images of yesteryear deserved to be available to a larger public audience, and this book aims to do just that. In order to provide a complete historical panorama of the London Fire Brigade, the book also includes modern prints of the London Fire Brigade at work at various fire and rescue incidents right up to the new millennium.

I must point out, however, that this book is not a definitive history of the London Fire Brigade but simply my very personal selection of those prints which seem to encapsulate the vivid life and times of London's firefighters since the early eighteenth century. I do hope that my work might further create more interest and appreciation of the historical background of one of the world's greatest fire brigades.

ACKNOWLEDGEMENTS

I would firstly like to thank London's Chief Fire Officer, Brian Robinson, without whose encouragement this book would not have been conceived. Then to my good friend Gordon White, London Fire Brigade Press Officer, Colin Williamson and Barbara Hyde of the LFB Press Office for their patient help with a number of the prints used in the book; Judy Seaborne and Graham De Core of the LFB Library and Photographic Archives; Pauline Drummond and Phil More of the LFB Photographic Processing Section; and fellow former LFB firefighter Ron Bentley, nowadays the Fire Safety Manager of the Palace of Westminster. Lastly, my sincere appreciation is due to my dear and long-suffering wife Susie, who has worked tirelessly throughout a project which has, as usual, required her very considerable secretarial, organisational and word processing skills.

This fire in a rubber merchant's riverside warehouse in Shad Thames, SE1, on 8 October 1935 spread so rapidly that crews had to be withdrawn from the building and the fire fought externally. Protective jets are in play on all the surrounding premises while a reserve breathing apparatus crew awaits amid the tangle of hose lines. Note some new style cork helmets alongside the brass versions.

INTRODUCTION

F ire is one of mankind's oldest enemies. Indeed, one does not have to delve too deeply to see that fire has often played an important part across the pages of the capital's history. London suffered great fires in 798 and 982, largely owing to the combustible nature of buildings and the use of naked flames. In 989 one of the largest fires to afflict London was described as 'so great and lamentable a fire that, beginning in Aldgate, it burned down houses and churches all the way from Ludgate together with the stately Fabrick of St Paul's'.

After the Norman invasion a law required fires and lights to be extinguished at nightfall, but major fires continued to occur, causing death, injury and widespread damage to growing London and its inhabitants. The first Great Fire of London broke out in 1212 and caused over 3,000 deaths. The 1666 Great Fire burned for four days and destroyed 13,000 homes, 84 churches and 44 livery halls, together with many other buildings. The fiscal damage of the fire was put at £10m, a huge sum in those times.

At the time of the 1666 Great Fire firefighting in London was mainly undertaken by bucket-chain volunteers, at best disorganised and largely ineffective against the regular ravages of life and property by fire. But in the aftermath of the 1666 Great Fire, the first public demand was voiced for a single organised fire brigade for London. However, it was still a slow path towards harnessing organisational skills and the available mechanical power to create some semblance of organised firefighting. This initially came about through the efforts of the first insurance companies' fire brigades in the late eighteenth century.

The modern-day London Fire Brigade (LFB) was born directly from the grouping of the largest insurance fire brigades in 1832 into the London Fire Engine Establishment (LFEE). Today's LFB is one of the largest all-professional fire brigades in the world. This book traces in photographic form the development of the capital's firefighting force from 1832 through three centuries of fire and rescue work, in both peace and war.

Even the most cursory look at the historical workload of London's firefighters readily illustrates the staggering growth of the demands upon London's fire brigade and its crews. In 1833, its first year of operation, the LFEE consisted of some eighty firemen of the twelve constituent insurance companies' fire brigades, operating from nineteen fire stations and two Thames fire floats. In its first year of operation the LFEE answered 592 calls. Contrast this with the year 1999–2000, when the 5,900 firefighters of the modern day LFB based at 113 fire stations responded to over 175,000 separate '999' incidents.

Most of the photographs used in the book were taken by LFB photographers and their work captures a truly remarkable story. The landmark years of the horse-drawn manual pumps, the arrival of steam power, the first motorised fire engines and considerable technical development in firefighting techniques and equipment were all well captured by the lens. So too are the dramatic years of the Second World War, when firefighters had a front-line role during the 1940–1 Blitz and the 1944–5 rocket attacks, probably some of the fieriest times in London's entire history.

Over the last fifty years the LFB has continued to develop its skills, expertise and equipment to meet the ever-widening firefighting and rescue challenges faced by London's firefighters, day and night, in all weather. For despite all the sophistication of modern-day technology, firefighting is still a difficult and dangerous profession. After all, fire crews usually enter smoke-filled buildings and other places of danger from where everyone else is fleeing.

Whether the focus is upon the days of leather and brass helmets of the nineteenth century, or right up to date on today's men and women who crew the LFB's front-line fire engines, it can truly be said that theirs is a special, even a noble calling. The challenging task of saving life and property from fire across the London area is in very good hands.

Neil Wallington
Bourne, Lincolnshire
June 2001

1 ORIGINS

The formation of the London Fire Brigade (LFB) can be clearly traced to the aftermath of the 1666 Great Fire of London and the enormous damage it caused. During the time immediately after the huge fire, moves were made to set up the first 'fire office' to insure buildings and contents against fire loss, the Phoenix. However, this fire office took so many claims in the 1680s that it became insolvent. This did not stop other insurance companies from coming forward, and in 1699 the Hand in Hand Fire Office took a memorable decision to form its own fire brigade.

Over the next decade others followed suit, so that by the early eighteenth century there were a number of insurance fire brigades in London, ready to respond with manual fire pumps to any property fire insured with their company, indicated by a metal fire plaque on the face of the building.

The first insurance company firemen were almost exclusively drawn from Thames watermen, paid a small retaining fee and a further sum for attendance at each fire. Colourful uniforms were provided although these were hardly practical for the rigours of firefighting.

Over the next century insurance fire brigades co-existed in London, but as the capital began to grow during the early part of the Industrial Revolution, competition between the individual insurance companies became intense. It had long been established that a brigade would only tackle a fire if the affected property was insured with that company. Rival brigades started openly to interfere and impede the efforts of other company fire crews. Slashing of fire hoses was not unknown and fighting often broke out. By 1830 the number of reliable fire pumps available in London had surprisingly dropped to thirty-eight. Clearly something had to be done.

After months of discussions it was proposed that the largest insurance company fire brigades should join forces and form one single unified fire brigade for the London area. These ten companies were the Alliance, Atlas, Globe, Imperial, London Assurance, Protector, Royal Exchange, Sun, Union and Westminster.

Final details were agreed in mid-1832. The new enlarged firefighting force would be known as the London Fire Engine Establishment (LFEE) and would embrace all the nineteen fire stations of the ten merging companies. Two river Thames floating fire stations would also be provided to cope with the immense fire risk in London's dockland. The first year's budget was to be £8,000, and interestingly, the LFEE's main purpose was to save property, with any saving of life to be incidental.

With headquarters in Watling Street in the heart of the insurance sector of the City, the LFEE came into being on 1 January 1833 and the origins of the modern-day LFB were born.

Around the time of the Great Fire of 1666 firefighting efforts were still fairly primitive, including hooks, bucket and chains and manual pumps. This contemporary print illustrates a hand-held squirt in use.

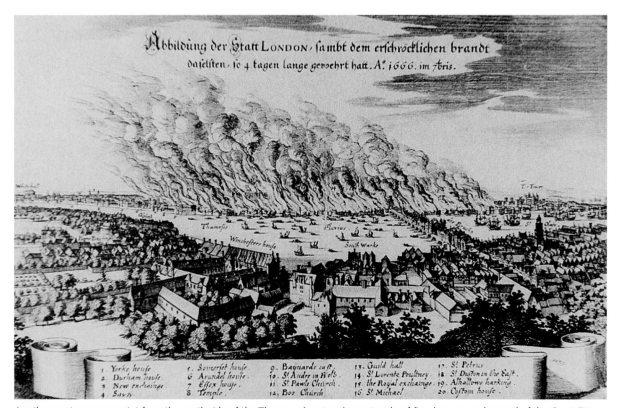

Another contemporary print from the south side of the Thames, showing the vast scale of fire damage and spread of the Great Fire.

This Hogarth cartoon of 1750 shows the chaos surrounding
the efforts of the Union Insurance firemen, and hindrance and
interference from various rival insurance fire brigades.

For many years insurance companies provided some fine
colourful liveries for their firemen, but gave little thought to the
practical necessities of the personal protection of their crews.

Insurance companies affixed metal 'firemarks' to the outside face of a building to identify an insured premises; in the event of a fire, only that insurance company fire brigade would extinguish any outbreak. From top: Norwich, Sun and Phoenix firemarks.

2 FOUNDING FATHERS

Once the London Fire Engine Establishment (LFEE) was conceived as London's unified firefighting organisation from 1 January 1833, the command of the new brigade was offered to, and accepted by, a Scotsman, James Braidwood. He was the 32-year-old Fire Master of Edinburgh and a surveyor by profession, and Braidwood had established a reputation as a dedicated leader of the Edinburgh fire insurance firefighters. He took firemen's training and fitness very seriously, often turning his crews out in the early hours to drill in the streets of Edinburgh. Braidwood claimed that he could have a manual pump turned out and coupled up to three lengths of hose in a little over a minute.

Nor was Braidwood desk-bound. At one Scottish fire he single-handedly saved nine persons from a fiery death. He also wrote the first British pamphlet on fire engine construction and designed a style of escape ladder which was to remain in universal use for many years.

Braidwood moved to London in 1833 on a salary of £400 per year and very quickly organised the nineteen fire stations of the LFEE into four districts. He soon provided a practical firefighting uniform for his men and introduced a standard manual pump for LFEE use. Over the next two decades, Braidwood built up a deserved reputation as a leader of men and became a pioneer in many aspects of firefighting technique and equipment.

The LFEE chief's sudden end came during a large Thameside warehouse blaze in Tooley Street on 22 June 1861. Braidwood was in the thick of it with his firemen when a gable end wall suddenly fell, killing him and one of his men instantly. Braidwood's funeral was one of the largest seen by Londoners for years. The procession was 1½ miles long and every church in the city tolled a bell.

The fatal Tooley Street fire caused immense damage and destruction and disrupted a significant part of London's import and export trade. A quarter mile stretch of collapsed and burnt-out riverside warehouses gave testament to a direct fire loss in excess of £2 million. For a while rumours in the City were rife that many insurance companies were on the brink of ruin as a result of claims. Even the payments to the voluntary civilian pumpers of the manual fire engines who gave some relief to the hard-pressed LFEE firemen totalled £1,100.

Soon after Braidwood's tragic death a Parliamentary Select Committee was set up to look at the fast-growing fire cover needs for London. By April 1862 the committee recommended the formation of a larger fire brigade for London under a scheme approved by the Secretary of State.

However, while Parliament was still deliberating the LFEE looked for a successor to Braidwood and late in 1861 finally appointed Eyre Massey Shaw, a 31-year-old ex-Irish army officer. Shaw was to prove a worthy successor to Braidwood and his achievements.

This document certifies the attendance of three manually pumped fire engines at a fire in the City of London on 21 October 1833. The first and third engines were from the newly created LFEE.

Appointed the first Superintendent of the LFEE in 1833, James Braidwood came from Edinburgh where he had been Firemaster for almost ten years.

The first real significant test of the LFEE's ability was the huge fire at the Palace of Westminster, 16 October 1834. Although both chambers (Lords and Commons) were destroyed, Westminster Hall was saved from serious damage. (*Fire Protection Association*)

A contemporary print showing the huge fire at the Palace of Westminster on 16 October 1834 and the renowned fire dog, Chance, pawing at a fire plug in the water mains. Chance was befriended by firemen at the LFEE at Watling Street in the City; he would run alongside the pumps at a turnout and generally follow the fire crews at the scene. Sadly Chance died under the wheels of a pump after some ten years of service.

A fireman of the LFEE.

A number of private fire brigades still continued to exist in London despite the growing strength and reliability of the LFEE. One of the principal private brigades was that of the Hodges Gin Distillery in Lambeth, inaugurated in 1851. Forty distillery employees manned two pumps. Formed initially to protect the Hodges buildings, the brigade soon started to respond to 'public' calls of fire, often beating Braidwood's firemen to the scene. Hodges was first to use steam pumps in 1863 and his steamer named *Torrent* became famous across the country for its powerful performance.

On the night of 10 January 1838 a huge fire severely damaged the Royal Exchange in the City of London. This contemporary print shows firefighting in progress with two powerful LFEE manual pumps at work (left to right foreground). Note the eight-a-side 'pumpers' in action toiling to provide a single firefighting jet, and the occupants of several nearby buildings threatened by firespread removing their valuables (centre).

The great riverside fire at Tooley Street, close by Tower Bridge, where Braidwood was killed by a falling wall, 22 June 1861. Damage was estimated at over £2 million.

A contemporary magazine print marking Braidwood's death at the Tooley Street fire.

Following Braidwood's death London's next fire chief was an Irishman, Captain (later Sir) Eyre Massey Shaw. Within four years the LFEE would become London's first municipally funded fire brigade, known as the Metropolitan Fire Brigade (MFB), and in 1866 Shaw was the natural choice to head London's new brigade.

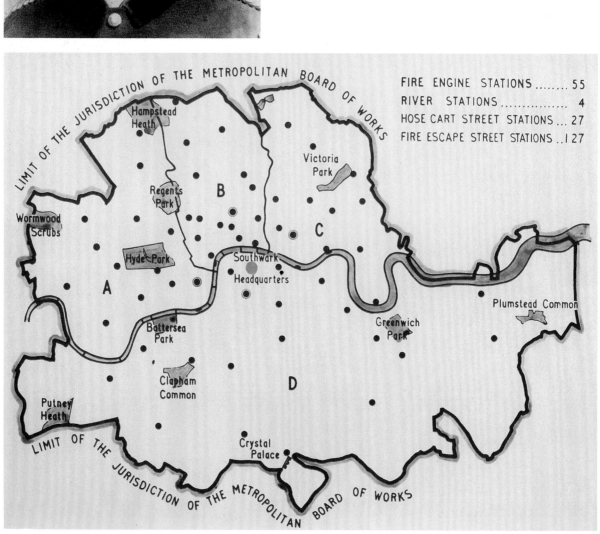

A map showing the location of MFB stations, 1 January 1889.

To the Rescue!

The hectic gallop to a fire. A Victorian image of a steamer pump of the MFB, en route to a fire call, *c.* 1875. Note the flying sparks from the chimney, and the fireman on the left calling out for all he is worth to warn the traffic ahead.

Four historic fire engines and a 50ft escape ladder pictured in the London Fire Brigade museum at Southwark, 8 June 1995. From the left: an early eighteenth-century manual of the parish of Mortlake, a curricle, *c.* 1870, manuals, *c.* 1838 and 1800, a typical hand-pushed escape ladder, *c.* 1850.

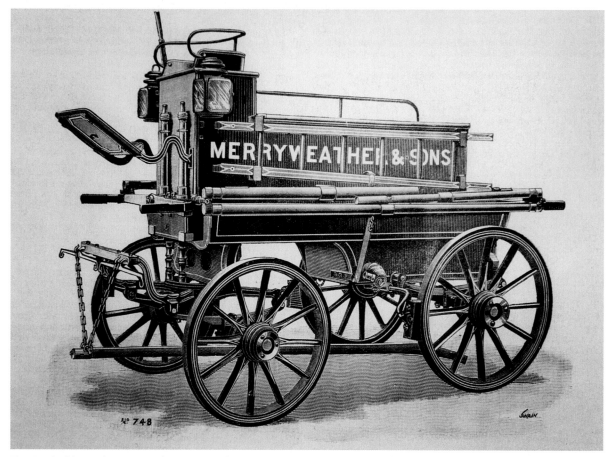

The standard horse-drawn manual pumping appliance of the MFB was manufactured by Merryweather. This basic design went back to 1851 and was pumped by the manual effort of up to thirty persons applied to long folding handles on each side. The pump needed to be supplied with water from a water main 'fire plug' or by bucket chain. It could deliver approximately 80 gallons per minute on to a fire through two leather hose lines.

Victorian hero. The epitome of a fireman's work is immortalised in this famous 1890 painting by Charles Vigor of a rescue by the MFB, simply entitled *Saved*. The setting is generally accepted as being on the steps of Winchester House, Massey Shaw's MFB headquarters in Southwark. The original painting now hangs in the dining hall of the Fire Service College in Gloucestershire.

In Chief Fire Officer Massey Shaw's days, potential recruits to the MFB had to pass a strength test: this involved raising a wheeled escape ladder into the vertical via a block and tackle arrangement. Here a candidate is on the top of the ladder, about to test his strength. The pull required a direct force of 244lbs and was clearly not an easy task.

After the creation of the MFB in 1866 the insurance companies relinquished their direct interest in the provision of fire brigades. However, at that time they did agree to create three corps of salvage men in London, Liverpool and Glasgow, who would attend fires to mitigate damage to business stock and fittings. Although called upon to work closely with firemen, the Salvage Corps took no part in firefighting. The three corps were finally disbanded in 1982. Here a London Salvage Corps crew hurry to the scene of a fire in Westminster, *c.* 1905.

3 THE FIRE KING

Eyre Massey Shaw quickly got into his stride as London's fire chief. He had received a strong education in scientific and mechanical topics and army service gave him further experience. However, Shaw was an independent spirit and throughout his command of London's fire brigade he was regularly at odds with politicians, usually over funding issues.

Shaw inherited seventeen LFEE land fire stations and was soon embroiled with the fire committee in the detail of the scheme for the proposed enlarged brigade. Under considerable pressure to keep the overall budget down, Shaw finally produced a plan for a fire brigade for the enlarged area of London protecting 117 square miles of the growing city. This embraced an area from Hampstead in the north, Bow in the east, Norwood in the south and Hammersmith and Putney in the west. This was the area covered by the London local authority, the Metropolitan Board of Works. Shaw envisaged forty-three fire stations manned by 232 professional firefighters, including many of the old LFEE crews.

On 1 January 1866 an Act brought the Metropolitan Fire Brigade (MFB) into being with Shaw as its Chief Officer. No parish pumps were allowed within the area of the MFB, although fire cover on the growing outer edges of the London conurbation still continued to rely upon mostly volunteer fire brigades.

Braidwood had surprisingly ignored steam-powered fire pumps even though these had first been perfected some thirty years earlier. Shaw soon introduced the first steam pumps in the brigade and also improved his firemen's firefighting rig, introducing a brass helmet to replace the leather version. Shaw ensured that horses for the MFB were specially bred for strength and speed; most London fire stations had five pairs of horses, two pairs being 'on call' at any one time.

Shaw rapidly became an international expert on fire prevention, especially in theatres and places of public assembly, where there had already been several fire disasters.

That the enlarged MFB was busy was not in doubt. In 1877 the MFB attended 5,452 separate fire calls, of which 4,021 were small to medium outbreaks; some 159 calls developed into major blazes.

By then Massey Shaw had become a member of London society, and in 1875 a London Auxiliary Fire Brigade was founded, something of a gentlemen's club which followed the fortunes of Shaw's brigade. Edward, Prince of Wales had a personal fire uniform kept ready at Chandos Street Fire Station, near Charing Cross, and for many years Shaw would send a carriage for the heir to the throne when there was a serious fire in progress. On these occasions the Prince of Wales was living dangerously; at one fire in 1887 the Prince was close to a wall which suddenly fell and killed a fireman and seriously injured two others. Whether Queen Victoria was aware of her son's hazardous pursuit is not known, but in 1883 Shaw was summoned by her to pronounce on the fire safety of the royal palaces.

Massey Shaw and the London Brigade were commemorated by Gilbert and Sullivan in their 1882 operetta *Iolanthe*. The words of a chorus ask the question: 'Oh! Captain Shaw. . . . Can thy Brigade with cold cascade quench my great love I wonder?'

This print captures all the high
drama and excitement of an
MFB turnout and dash to a fire,
c. 1870.

Victorian fire scene, *c.* 1890. The crew
of a horse-drawn steam pump of the
MFB gets to work watched by a large
crowd. (*Fire Protection Association*)

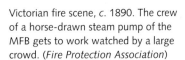

A scale model of an MFB Shand Mason single-cylinder steam pump, *c.* 1890, showing the fine array of brass and copper work. Capable of delivering up to 200 gallons per minute, these pumps could provide powerful firefighting water jets.

IN MEMORY OF GEORGE LEE, A FIREMAN OF THE METROPOLITAN FIRE BRIGADE, WHO DIED ON THE 7TH OF AUGUST 1876, OF INJURIES RECEIVED WHILST GALLANTLY ENGAGED IN SAVING THE LIVES OF OTHER PERSONS AT A FIRE AT No 97 St. JOHN St. WEST SMITHFIELD, ON THE 26TH OF JULY 1876. THE METROPOLITAN BOARD OF WORKS CAUSED THIS TABLET TO BE AFFIXED.

A memorial plate commemorating the gallant actions of MFB Fireman George Lee.

The destruction by fire of St Mary Magdalene, Knightrider Street, off Queen Victoria Street, City of London, 8 December 1886.

Three MFB crews pose on the forecourt of Southwark Headquarters, c. 1895. Two steamer pumps (left and right) flank a 50ft wheeled escape. The accommodation above the station is pretty spartan family flats, and one young fireman's daughter looks down from a third floor window.

Part of the MFB's River Thames firefighting provision, *c.* 1870.
The fire tug *Antelope* positions a fire float for an attack on a
warehouse fire. The float has a steam pump capable of taking
2 tons of water per minute from the river for about eight
firefighting jets.

A Victorian image of the bravery of the MFB. Two firemen
snatch a family trapped by fire and smoke to safety down an
escape ladder.

An early pattern Merryweather manual pump, manufactured especially for the MFB, *c.* 1870. Captain Shaw considered that fifteen men on each side produced the optimum firefighting water performance of about 80 gallons per minute on to the fire.

A horse-drawn 50ft wheeled escape ladder and five-man crew in Southwark Headquarter's drill yard, *c.* 1890. These escape ladders could be very quickly 'slipped' by the crew and extended up to a window. Their sole role was rescue, and these units, one of which was based at each fire station, carried no firefighting equipment. Note the lack of warning devices to help them through London's traffic throng – the crew would shout 'Hi! Hi! Hi!' to clear the way. The fireman on the left has his right hand on the brake lever and would operate this during the exciting dash to the fire.

By the start of the twentieth century horse power was still the predominant motive power of the Brigade. Most horses were provided by Tilling's, the London bus company, and for many years the horses were specially bred for the Metropolitan and London Fire Brigades. Pairs were allocated to stations where they usually spent their entire working lives tended by a brigade coachman. The horses were spoilt and loved by firemen and public alike.

A newspaper print of the MFB stables inside a London fire station, showing the horses harnessed up ready for a fire call to come in.

An historic and sad occasion for the LFB in November 1921, when the Brigade bade farewell to the last horse-drawn fire engine in the capital – the turntable ladder attached to Kensington Fire Station.

4 STEAM POWER

Steam-powered fire engines became available from about 1830 onwards, although both the LFEE and the MFB continued to rely upon manually pumped fire engines until Massey Shaw introduced the first horse-drawn steam pump in 1865. Manual pumps relied upon the physical efforts of firemen or volunteers from the watching crowd; the latter usually expected reward either by copious supplies of beer, or cash payment, or both!

The first London steamers, all single-cylinder models, relieved the Brigade's dependence upon manual pumping, although this method continued to supplement London steam pump firefighting operations until as late as 1899.

Throughout the nineteenth century two makers of steamer fire engines dominated the scene, Merryweather and Shand Mason. Over the years both companies supplied the MFB until horse-drawn fire engines were finally replaced upon the onset of an all-motor pumping fleet in 1919.

However, twenty years earlier steam power led directly to the first self-propelled fire engines in the MFB. In 1899 Merryweather patented their Fire King model. This used steam to power the fire engine up to a maximum of 12 mph. At 5½ tons, the Fire King was a bit of a monster, and its braking performance left much to be desired. Although the Brigade introduced ten Fire Kings, by the turn of the century battery- and petrol-powered fire engines were already on the horizon.

Steam pumps were usually in the care of an engineer. Boiler water was always kept warm in the fire stations by oil burners under the boiler, and later on by gas rings, and the fire was always laid with kindling. Once a call came in the firebox contents were ignited, and such was the clever design of boiler flues that steam was raised even after the short gallop to a fire scene. There the horses would be unhitched, and with the steam pump quickly connected up to a water main, firefighting jets were soon at work.

Later models of steam pump came in two-cylinder compound versions, using steam at high and low pressure, and were even more powerful than the earlier models. All the steam pumps were beautifully mechanically balanced machines, and would pump reliably for hours on end. Like the Brigade's horses, the steamer pumps were immaculately kept and cared for with their gleaming brass and copperwork fittings always highly polished.

Occasionally one of these 120-year-old veterans now in preservation is wheeled out for display purposes, as at several royal visits of recent years. On these occasions they are still so efficient that they are able to project water jets to a height sometimes unmatched by that from the latest turbo diesel fire engines!

In 1899 Merryweather modified its steamer pumps to also propel the vehicle, and thus London's first non-horse-drawn fire engines arrived. Unfortunately the Fire Kings, as they were called, were slow (12 mph maximum) and cumbersome to steer. Stopping was also a problem as they weighed some 5½ tons. This photograph was taken at Southwark Headquarters in 1905.

The Fire King was, however, an efficient pumping unit, and here a crew prepare to get a hose line to work during a drill session at Southwark, 1905.

Over 100 years ago the Brigade encouraged a good public image, often opening its doors to exercises and special training events. Here a Saturday afternoon summer display at Southwark Headquarters draws an attentive boater-hatted crowd. A horse-drawn steamer (centre) works two firefighting jets alongside an early motor pump, while a horse-drawn turntable ladder (left) is fully extended to 85ft.

At the turn of the century serious efforts were being made by the Brigade to provide reliable breathing equipment to allow fire crews to get inside smoke-filled buildings. Here a crew at Southwark Headquarters, *c.* 1903, practise smoke helmet drill with the wearer connected to a fresh air pump (right).

In 1904 the Metropolitan Fire Brigade changed its name to the London Fire Brigade. Less than one year later it was possible for crews to call in to Southwark Headquarters from a remote point, using a street fire alarm call point. In this way urgent requests for assistance could be relayed, as well as information about firefighting operations and general back-up support required, especially at major fires.

LFB fire station pets, 1904. Two parrots, one monkey, three dogs and a cat make up a fine collection.

Redcross Street, Barbican, EC1: a typical London fire station, pictured *c.* 1905. By then the MFB had become the London Fire Brigade, a title carried through to the present day. The escape ladder and its immaculate greys pose on the forecourt. Alongside is the Station Officer in charge (and his dog) while inside the engine house is a steam pump and hose cart. Above the engine house is the spartan family accommodation necessary to support the continuous duty system of that era.

By the turn of the century the Brigade was also experimenting with electric vehicles. This Cedes battery-driven pump and escape carrier was one of a number in use when this picture was taken in July 1905. Eighty-four batteries weighing 2½ tons were housed under the long bonnet (slid open in this view). These electric pumps were slow and required lots of attention when on charge, and were quickly overtaken by the new petrol pumps soon to arrive on the scene. Note the anti-skid plates on the tyres.

A Shand Mason steamer ready
for the turnout, Manchester
Square Fire Station, *c.* 1906.
This is a more powerful two-
cylinder model. Water in the
boiler was kept warm by a small
gas ring. The fire was laid ready
in the firebox and could be
ready to provide steam within
five minutes after turnout.
Immaculate brass helmets hang
ready on the left.

Around the turn of the nineteenth century the Thames fire risk, particularly that in the Pool of London and Dockland, was such that
the MFB introduced several new fireboats. Here, with Tower Bridge in the background, the Brigade's new fireboat, *Beta*, prepares to
show off her firefighting capability. With a draught of only 19in, the *Beta* could still operate at very low tides. Note the forward-
mounted powerful firefighting monitor.

By 1900 a number of new fire stations were being opened across London and many were substantial and elegant buildings. Manchester Square is in Chiltern Street, W1. This was a 'district' station supervising the work of eighteen fire stations and also provided family accommodation for many firemen on call.

This 1910 view of a manual pump attached to Thornton Heath Fire Station of Croydon Fire Brigade makes for an interesting comparison. Croydon was a small municipal brigade on the southern edge of the LFB area. Although they acquired a steamer pump in late Victorian times, in 1910 they were obviously still relying on manual pumps as part of their firefighting armoury. In 1965 the four fire stations of the Croydon Brigade, including Thornton Heath, became part of the enlarged Greater London Fire Brigade.

This six-man LFB crew attached to Dulwich Fire Station pose on the forecourt with their Merryweather steam pump, *c.* 1905. One member of a fireman's family peers through the lace curtains of the accommodation at first-floor level.

5   THE MOTOR AGE

The coming of the motorised fire engine, firstly steam powered, then battery driven, and finally petrol powered, truly heralded a new age of technical development for the LFB. Motor fire engines gave fire crews the ability to get to the scene of fires somewhat faster than horses, and to carry more firefighting and rescue equipment.

Up to the mid-1930s all workhorse motor pumps were completely open to the weather. Each vehicle had outward-facing seats for the crew down each side with a handrail for the firemen to hang on to. Little wonder that down the years quite a few injuries (and the occasional death) were caused as the fire engine swung around corners at speed and a crew member was thrown off. In 1934 the LFB introduced the first new pumps with transverse crew seating. This series of open fire engines remained in front line service in London until 1955.

By 1920 new all-steel turntable ladders were able to reach up to 100ft, about seven floors height, giving firemen much quicker access up to people trapped above an outbreak of fire by smoke and flames.

Breathing apparatus, too, was another area of radical improvement, with special crews beginning to be dedicated to penetrating the interior of smoke-filled buildings wearing their one-hour duration oxygen sets. Even so, the old culture of a 'good' fireman being one who could work without a breathing set and able to take the regular respiratory punishment of the fireground died hard.

However, with the steady growth in 'special service' calls – to emergencies other than fire, particularly road crashes – the Brigade's emergency tenders were carrying more specialist rescue equipment such as cutting gear, and more powerful jacking and floodlighting equipment.

The training programmes for officers and firemen also continued to improve and expand. Indeed, the LFB was readily recognised as one of the leading fire brigades in the world, often borne out by the number of London officers who went on to command other brigades at home and abroad.

Despite the difficult industrial climate in the run up to the General Strike, in 1925 all professional firemen began to receive pension rights with an ill health and serious injury provision. By then, the London firemen's working week had been reduced from 144 hours to 72 on a new shift system.

Recruitment into the Brigade was keenly contested and the necessary physical strength and mental tests often meant that only one in 100 applicants was accepted into training school, with ex-sailors continuing to be preferred. By the mid-1930s the LFB was truly something of an elite corps, yet one which was shortly to face its most fearsome and lengthy examination by fire in the entire history of the capital city.

One of the first motorised fire engines used by the LFB, *c.* 1909. This was a Merryweather Hatfield pump capable of 30 mph. A normal crew would be up to six firemen: for the photographer the entire station duty watch have climbed aboard!

This 10–12hp car chassis was purchased in 1903 and converted in Brigade workshops to run as a first aid and firefighting tender.

Rear Admiral James de Courcy Hamilton became Chief of the Brigade in 1903 and relentlessly drove forward motorisation. Here is his own driver and steam-powered car, the first motorised vehicle to be owned by the Brigade, pictured outside Southwark Fire Station.

This classic picture shows one of the LFB's first emergency tenders, introduced in 1904. These Dennis fire engines carried the first breathing apparatus sets and various lighting equipment, together with some basic lifting and metal cutting tools likely to be needed at non-fire emergencies that were beginning to occur at that time. This emergency tender was based at Clerkenwell Fire Station.

A Cedes battery-driven pump/50ft escape, based at Bow Fire Station and pictured in the drill yard at Southwark Headquarters, *c.* 1906. Batteries stowed under the bonnet added 2½ tons to the total vehicle weight. Although battery power did not last long in the LFB, the emerging shape of the early twentieth-century fire engine is clearly there.

The successful use of radio was well established in the Brigade by 1907, and this view of the watchroom at Streatham Fire Station shows the radio equipment ready for use.

Unprotected steel columns fail very early during the high temperatures of large fires. Here is the tangled web of girders following a serious fire at Woolwich Arsenal, 18 April 1906.

Firemen work amid part of the collapsed Arding and Hobbs department store at Clapham Junction during damping down and salvage work, 20 December 1909. Surprisingly, they have dispensed with their brass helmets, despite the obvious risk of falling debris all around.

The watchroom of Southwark Fire Station, *c.* 1909. Although this had a telephone switchboard serving the adjacent headquarters of the Brigade, technology is clearly beginning to make the job of answering fire calls from street fire alarms a more effective one.

King Edward VII had, as Prince of Wales, always been interested in the MFB and its work, often covertly going to fires with Captain Massey Shaw. Once he was monarch this sometimes dangerous activity ceased, but King Edward did continue his support for London's firemen. Here he, Queen Alexandra and the royal children arrive for the 1909 Annual Brigade Review in Hyde Park. Note the brass helmeted young prince. These were major public events where the Brigade, by then the LFB, would perform drills and parade past the monarch, after which the King and Queen would present gallantry and long-service medals.

At the 1909 Annual Review in Hyde Park, the King, no doubt mindful of his firefighting days some thirty years earlier with Massey Shaw, presented gallantry awards, while the Queen gave out long-service medals. This print shows the scene towards the end of the medal ceremony, which had been preceded by a dazzling drill display by twenty-four galloping steamer pumps and ladder units going through various firefighting and rescue evolutions.

After the medal presentation at the 1909 Royal Review in Hyde Park the crowds were allowed to inspect the assembled lines of immaculate fire engines of the LFB. Many thousands of Londoners turned out for this Review, and here the throng completely engulfs the rows of uniformed firemen and their equipment. Each pair of Brigade horses needed to be on their best behaviour during this major London social event.

This Leyland foam tender was introduced in 1910 to provide a reliable quantity of firefighting foam, which was required to tackle fires in petrol or oil installations.

By the outbreak of the First World War the LFB area was well covered with electric street fire alarms. On breaking the glass cover, the brass handle was pulled and this would register at the fire station the precise location of the alarm. The instruction on the alarm says 'Wait For Engine', so that the caller could then direct the crew into action.

The horses were the particular pride of the LFB and were spoilt and cossetted by the fire station crews. Coachmen were encouraged to enter their horses in national competitions, and here a first prize for working horses has been won by these fine steeds attached to Holborn Fire Station, and in the care of Head Coachman Albert Thacker, on 24 June 1911.

Apart from public displays at Southwark Headquarters, the Brigade also staged regular events in and around the London area. Here a coachman and his crew put their steamer pump into a tight turn against the clock during a driving competition in Victoria Park, east London, c. 1911.

An early motor pump of the LFB pictured in Caledonian Road Fire Station, N1, *c.* 1913. Note the transverse-mounted water deliveries, large warning bell and the 12 miles per hour marking!

Cannon Street Fire Station, *c.* 1915, showing both horse-drawn (centre) and motorised (far left and right) pumps. The far pump is a battery-electric: these were tried in the Brigade for several years before the move to an all-petrol fleet. Note the suspended horse harness above the draw bar, ready for quick connection to the horses waiting in the stables nearby.

This Cedes 75ft turntable ladder (TL) was one of several which entered LFB service in 1914. Driven by two front axle-mounted 180 volt, 18hp motors, this type of TL saw eleven years' action before being superseded by more modern petrol-driven 100ft versions.

The motorised age comes to the LFB, Southwark, September 1909. This petrol Merryweather/Hatfield chain-driven pump could deliver 500 gallons of water per minute at the fire and travel at 30 mph! Note the ubiquitous hose cart in the background (left).

The crew of Clerkenwell Fire Station's emergency tender pose for the camera in their one-hour duration oxygen Proto breathing apparatus sets. When this picture was taken in 1919 self-contained breathing apparatus for firefighting was still in its early stages. This would be an experienced crew of firefighters who would be called in at major fires when breathing apparatus was deemed to be necessary. Note the petrol-engined generator mounted on the rear of the vehicle to provide floodlighting for night-time incidents.

A view of the LFB's first breakdown lorry, commissioned in 1919. This Dennis had a rear-mounted crane and various sheerlegs to allow for sewer and other line rescues, and was based at Southwark Headquarters.

By 1919 self-contained firefighting breathing apparatus (BA) sets were becoming available and the LFB introduced several special tenders to provide a rapid response to serious fires where deep penetration into the smoke was required. Here, Clerkenwell's BA tender parades with its crew and some of its specialised equipment, including an early petrol lighting generator. The Proto one-hour BA sets used pure oxygen – note the spare oxygen cylinders on the running board.

The increasing need for ladders capable of reaching beyond the scope of the standard wheeled escape saw the introduction of the first horse-drawn turntable ladder in the late 1890s. By 1920, the time of this view, the LFB were using this style of 75ft powered ladder.

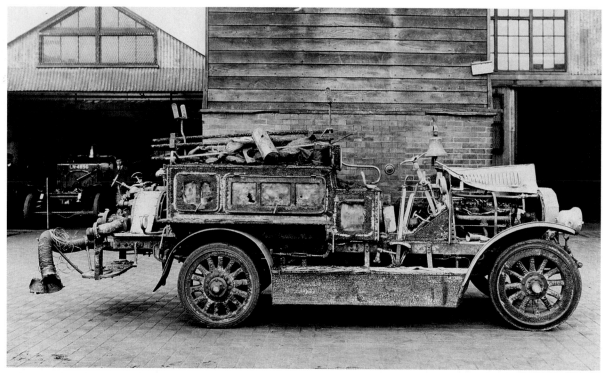

A dramatic fire took place on the night of 15 August 1920 on the Thames at Woolwich, south-east London. The barge *Dorcas*, laden with several thousand gallons of petrol, caught fire, burned through her mooring ropes and, drifting in the tide, blazed furiously. The *Dorcas* collided and set fire to two tugs, Woolwich Pier and nine other barges, a ferryboat and several buildings before grounding on the shore. By then ten LFB pumps were waiting, but as they got to work the *Dorcas* blew up with flames 300ft high. Although there were no serious injuries, firemen had to abandon three pumps which were all burnt out. Here are the remains of one.

The appliance room of Cannon Street Fire Station in the City, *c.* 1922. The horses are not long gone, and their empty stalls can be seen left of centre. A pump escape (top right) and a turntable ladder (top left) await the call to duty. Note the brass pole and the hose cart (right).

Southwark, the headquarters' fire station of the LFB up until the move to Lambeth in 1937. This view, taken in 1923, shows, from the left, a pump, pump escape, emergency tender, turntable ladder, foam tender and two support vans ready to go. The accommodation above is firemen's flats: they virtually lived above the job and their homes could be (and were) inspected for cleanliness at any time of the day or night by the duty senior officer!

By comparison, this 1928 view of Millwall Fire Station on the Isle of Dogs is typical of many smaller two-pump London stations. Note the brass fire bell call out point to the left of the turnout doors. Pulling this would ring the bells throughout the station and produce a very fast turnout.

An interesting view taken during damping down and clearing up operations following a twenty-pump fire at Sandersons Paper Factory, east London, 11 October 1928. The two crews probably have a watching brief to ensure that there is no re-ignition of the debris. Note the almost un-extended 50ft wheeled escape in use, together with a hook ladder at a higher level.

Here a 50ft escape ladder has been pitched to a third-floor loophole to enable the crew to get a hose line to work, Tanners Paperworks, Whitefriars Street, EC4, 15 March 1930. The hose, yet to be charged with water, has been laid out up the ladder, and once they have water these firemen will move into the smoke-filled top floor of the warehouse, just off Fleet Street, to seek out the fire.

In 1929 the Brigade introduced the first enclosed emergency tender to respond to large fires where breathing apparatus was needed, together with the first non-fire emergencies, including car and rail crashes and various mechanical accidents and human tragedy. The new emergency tenders, built upon a Dennis chassis and based at Lambeth and Clerkenwell, were travelling workshops and were the forerunners of today's modern fire service rescue tenders in use throughout the British Fire Service.

For some eighty years the Brigade had its own fine band, which consisted entirely of serving London firefighters, most of whom were talented musicians who had played in a band during naval or military service. Here the LFB Band performs at the 1929 Annual Review at Victoria Park in east London. Sadly the Band's day came to an end in the early 1970s when the number of musical firefighters dwindled.

Another view of part of the 1929 Annual Review. Here the be-medalled assembled crews raise their brass helmets in 'Three Cheers' for the reviewing officer, Lord Snell.

Firefighters always have an impish sense of humour, often required to offset frequent grim sights and experiences of the work of the fire service. Here the camera catches a lighter moment as a fireman poses alongside a statue of Queen Victoria amid the damage after a twenty-pump fire at the People's Palace Amusement Centre, Mile End Road, Stepney, E1, 25 February 1931.

The fire service has to work in all weathers and these London firemen not only look frozen but are well on the way to becoming completely iced up. This huge riverside warehouse fire broke out at Butlers Wharf, SE1, just below Tower Bridge, during a spell of very wintry weather, 9 March 1931. Firefighting operations were complicated by the below-zero temperatures: hose lines quickly became stiff with ice and the area all around the fire was treacherously slippery.

A long-gone LFB training routine. Jumping sheets were carried on front line London fire engines up to late 1941 when the wartime National Fire Service came about. Until then weekly drills with a fireman playing the 'jumper' took place. Here, during a 1931 display at Southwark, the command has gone out, 'Taut Sheet!' And down into the sheet comes a London fireman almost standing to attention.

A 'drop of thickers' would be a London firefighter's apt expression to describe this view of a roof fire in offices just off Farringdon Street, close by Holborn Viaduct railway station, 14 May 1932. No breathing apparatus sets are in evidence despite the dense, acrid smoke. This fire was caused by careless contractors using blow torches during plumbing work. Sadly this cause is not unknown today.

On 16 June 1932 the Brigade was called to the head office of the Prudential Assurance Company in High Holborn, WC1. This picture was taken several hours after a fire in a store room had been extinguished and crews were making up all their gear. At the time several window displays of the large Prudential building portrayed the benefits of insurance, and here two London firemen admire the 'Fire' advert.

Crowds have always been drawn to watch firefighters at work, but this is perhaps an extreme case. Several thousand city workers spend their lunchtime break spectating at this ten-pump fire in a shop and dwellings in Paul Street, EC2, 15 June 1936.

Damping down following a major fire is always a dirty and time consuming exercise, but an important one nevertheless. Firefighters must be confident that a fire is completely out before they leave the scene. When tons of waste paper are involved, as in this view, this becomes a laborious task – often necessitating relief crews to ease the burden of those firefighters who are tired from several hours of firefighting activity. This is the Salvation Army Depot, Spa Road, Bermondsey, SE16, on 6 July 1933.

A significant historical landmark was passed on 14 July 1934 when the Brigade started to replace its traditional brass helmets with a new compressed cork design. This in part came about following the death of a fireman when his brass helmet touched a live cable during firefighting operations. Here the old helmet, a symbol of firemen for over seventy years, meets a modern and safer replacement.

One of the many hazards to firefighters is the sudden collapse of high walls which become unsupported as building joists and columns weaken and fail in the high temperatures of a severe fire. Part of the science of firefighting is to watch for the signs of deterioration in a building structure. Fortunately all crews were clear when this huge warehouse wall came crashing down in Shepherd's Bush, W12, on 10 September 1934.

A crew rigged in Proto one-hour oxygen breathing apparatus sets descend into the smoking hold of the SS *Leopard* moored in the Pool of London, 18 October 1934. Fire has broken out deep inside the vessel and the first task is to find exactly where the fire is located under the stacked general cargo.

This upwind dramatic scene shows the early stages of firefighting at a serious blaze in offices in Farringdon Street, off Ludgate Circus, EC4, 16 November 1934. Two turntable ladders are at work; one as a rescue staircase for workers trapped at fourth- and fifth-floor levels, the second providing a powerful water jet. Amid the swirling smoke, other wheeled escape ladders have been pitched and firemen are battling inside to knock the fire down. Fifteen pumps and 100 firemen are in attendance and the incident control point has been set up at the emergency tender with a white roof (centre). Note the neat parking area on the right for both reinforcing pumps and senior officers' cars. Each of the latter is fitted with a large electric bell.

A fine action shot of the aerial attack from two 100ft turntable ladders, 16 November 1934. Fire has broken out on the fourth floor of this five-floor office building in Farringdon Street, EC4, and is spreading fast. Crews are also at work inside the building. Two office workers perished in the fire but about thirty trapped people were led down to safety.

Another view of the firefighting attack on the roof fire. Note that the top of the turntable ladder on the left is totally engulfed in the swirling black smoke: the fireman on the head of the ladder must be having a pretty rough time.

This interesting study was taken during the clearing up stages of a fifteen-pump fire in offices in Grand Buildings, Northumberland Avenue, just off Trafalgar Square, 3 July 1935. A pump is still at work in the left foreground, while a relief crew from the emergency tender (right) await a call to action. Two of the crew are ready rigged in breathing apparatus. Their hands held behind their backs suggests a military 'stand at ease' situation. In the background London's traffic gets back to normal.

An aerial view of one of the
Brigade's gleaming new Dennis
pumps introduced in 1934–5.
This pump saw service
throughout the London Blitz
and continued peacetime
service until withdrawn in 1955.

The new generation of Dennis motor pumps had forward-facing seats for the crew to avoid the increasing injury (and death) to
firemen often caused by them being thrown off the sides of pumps en route to fires. In winter the firemen would arrive at a fire scene
frozen stiff. These new Dennis pumps could carry either a 50ft wheeled escape ladder or a shorter extension ladder, as well as a host
of hose and other equipment. (*Fox Photos*)

Another view of one of the new 1935 Dennis pumps at Southwark Headquarters, with a crew getting a hose reel to work. The driver is engaging the water pump, which is fed from an inbuilt 100 gallon water tank.

In the same year the Brigade also commissioned a number of fully enclosed Leyland pumps. This one carries a 50ft escape with two 'snatch rescue' 13ft long hook ladders ready on top for use with hooks extended. The Leyland also carries the London County Council logo. Note the early use of radio (twin-mounted aerials), twin bells and amber warning lights, and the side-mounted water extinguisher. A truly classic fire engine of its day.

In 1935 the Brigade also replaced some ageing turntable ladders with Leyland/Merryweather 100ft all-steel versions. These were used not only for rescue up to seventh-floor height, but also to project firefighting water jets into burning buildings. This fireman has a superb view over the Southwark roof tops. (*Fox Photos*)

A typical big Thameside fire of the sort which the LFB had tackled for over 100 years: Colonial Wharf, Wapping High Street, E1, 27 September 1935. This nine-storey warehouse was full of crude rubber and burned for four days, during which time a number of explosions took place. Sixty pumps, twenty special appliances and three fireboats, manned in all by 600 firemen, fought the huge blaze: they successfully prevented firespread to the surrounding warehouses.

Some very hungry, thirsty and tired London firemen gather at the Brigade's canteen van following the Colonial Wharf fire. After hours of action the main body of the fire is out, but fresh crews will be on the scene for several days and nights to come. For the time being these firemen who formed the main firefighting attack force can relax, swap stories and enjoy the piping-hot cocoa and sandwiches. Note the brass helmet conveniently placed on the serving canopy.

A London fireman fully rigged for action, *c.* 1936, showing the new compressed cork helmet; this replaced the traditional brass helmets of the MFB that had been in use since 1866. The change came about because of the risk of electrocution with the brass helmet and the greater strength, protection and lightness offered by the new helmet. Nevertheless many London firemen bemoaned the loss of the shiny helmet, which had been a symbol for seventy years.

Below: This scene shows the later stages of firefighting operations at a serious blaze at the Surrey Commercial Docks, 7 March 1936. These crews have set up an intense water curtain to protect nearby unaffected buildings from radiated heat. The eight powerful jets are provided through radial branches: these were heavy tripods which incorporated large nozzles and relieved firemen of the tiring effort of holding a branch for hours on end, resisting the jet reaction forces. These eight jets are throwing about 2,000 gallons of water per minute. Note the two firemen (right) wearing the new cork helmets.

On 30 November 1936 London saw one of its largest fires for many years when the Crystal Palace in south London caught fire.

Towards the later stages of the Crystal Palace fire the Duke of Kent arrived to view operations. The Duke is seen here (left) with the Chairman of the LCC Fire Committee (centre) and the LFB Chief Fire Officer, Major Morris (right). Soon after this picture was taken Major Morris whisked the Royal visitor off to don fire kit, and then took him in close to see some of the seventy pumps at the scene and talk to a few of the 400 firemen at work on the huge site.

The aftermath of the huge fire at the Crystal Palace, south London, taken the morning after the fire, 1 December 1936. The massive area of total fire destruction is evident, with only about 10 per cent of the glass and iron structure of the 1851 Great Exhibition building left standing.

By the time of the First World War the LFB had a centralised control room from where all telephone emergency calls to the Brigade were received. With the opening of the Brigade's new Lambeth Headquarters in 1937 a new control centre was commissioned, and this was the nerve centre of the LFB's operations, using all the latest telecommunications equipment.

The tradition of Saturday afternoon headquarters' displays by the Brigade continued when the new Lambeth Headquarters was opened in 1937. Here, in an historical item, a crew puts a preserved horse-drawn steamer through its paces before an appreciative crowd.

One of the crew of a Shand Mason MFB steam pump stokes the rather inaccessible firebox before preparing for a demonstration drill at Lambeth Headquarters, 1938. By then brass helmets were purely for ceremonial occasions such as this. This Shand Mason was one of several steam pumps preserved by the LFB.

The Brigade's new headquarters on the Albert Embankment at Lambeth was opened by His Majesty King George VI and Queen Elizabeth on 21 July 1937. Here the King, accompanied by Chief Fire Officer Morris, reviews the smart lines of 100 representative firemen drawn from all the LFB's fire stations. The crews stationed at Lambeth parade in front of their fire engines behind. While the review proceeds, Queen Elizabeth receives a bouquet of flowers (far left).

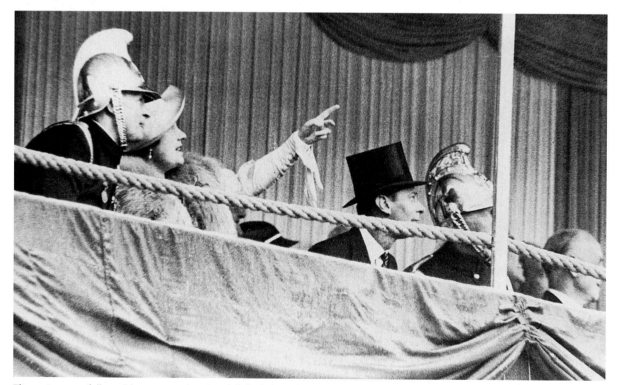

The review was followed by a comprehensive drill display involving pumps, wheeled escapes, hook ladders and firefighting rescue skills, culminating in a massed firefighting jets scene. Here Queen Elizabeth points out some special activity high up the drill tower, while the King looks similarly enthralled.

The morning after a serious fire caused damage to the HMV record shop in Oxford Street, W1, 27 December 1937. Through the determined efforts of over 150 firemen the buildings either side were saved.

The fire in the large HMV shop brought much of the West End of London to a halt. For four hours 150 firemen with thirty pumps fought to prevent the fire from spreading to the adjoining shops and offices. Here two pump operators supervise a complicated water relay where their pumps are taking water from large trunk mains at Oxford Circus, over half a mile away. Note the water board official on the right, known as a turncock. At large fires his job was to direct the maximum amount of water for LFB use.

Part of the Roll of Honour sculptured panels at LFB headquarters at Lambeth (see also p. 171).

6 FIREMEN AT WAR

As storm clouds gathered over Europe in the mid-1930s, it was clear that in the event of war fire brigades would be under severe pressure to deal with the effects of enemy aerial raiding.

Two separate Acts of Parliament underlined the urgency placed upon fire brigades, particularly those in the cities and urban areas. One Act, which became law in January 1938, authorised the formation of a volunteer firefighting force to be known as the Auxiliary Fire Service (AFS), whose role was to supplement the resources of regular fire brigades in the event of war.

By 1938 the peacetime establishment of the regular LFB was 2,500 officers and firemen based at fifty-eight land and three river stations across the London County Council area. The London AFS scheme envisaged supplying 28,000 men and women auxiliaries stationed at 360 sub-stations, mostly requisitioned premises such as schools and garages.

When war was declared on 3 September 1939 AFS recruitment was not yet up to these numbers, although by Christmas 1939 the training system was pretty full with AFS recruits undergoing a basic sixty-hour induction course before becoming full-time London auxiliaries.

But the war was slow to come to the Home Front. By the spring of 1940 the AFS were being termed 'army dodgers' and 'the darts and snooker brigade'. Then came the very first targeted air raid on London on the night of 7 September 1940; the London Blitz had begun. From that night onwards, the capital was unrelentingly raided on the following fifty-seven consecutive nights. The men and women of the AFS suffered a baptism of fire and came together with the regular LFB crews nightly to tackle fires of huge proportions, often with 2,000 pumps in attendance in one fire area alone. Water was always at a premium, often coming from fireboats pumping from the Thames, several miles away. For the first time firewomen were in the front line, manning canteen vans, control units, petrol carriers, and providing dispatch riders. The intense London Blitz lasted through to April 1941, with further sporadic heavy raids into late 1942.

During the early Blitz period it became evident that many fire brigades could not easily reinforce other hard-pressed regions owing to problems of incompatible equipment, different command structures and operational procedures. As a direct result, on 18 August 1941 the government unified all 1,600-odd UK fire brigades into the National Fire Service (NFS) under one common Home Office umbrella. Although the NFS was never really tested by fire, the London Region (largely the old LFB) had to deal with the massed V1 flying bomb and V2 rocket attacks of 1944–5 before peace finally arrived.

During the war years 327 London firemen and firewomen were killed on duty, and over 3,000 were seriously wounded while on firefighting operations. Churchill later said 'They were a grand lot and their work must never be forgotten.'

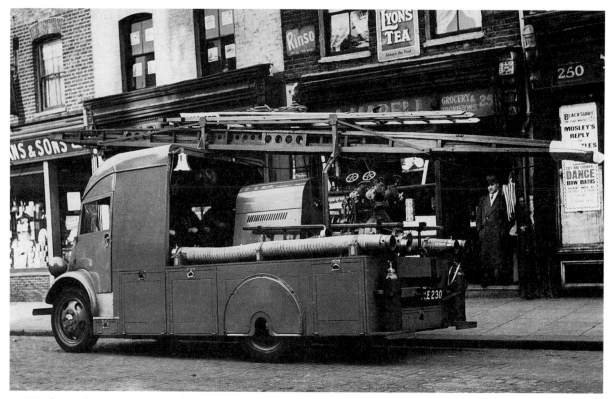

In 1938 the Auxiliary Fire Service (AFS) was set up to provide a reserve firefighting force in the event of a European war. AFS crews were allocated their own firefighting pumps provided by the Home Office. This London AFS Fordson/Sulzer heavy pump is pictured in Bethnal Green, east London, in March 1939. Finished in battleship grey, these AFS pumps were devoid of traditional brass and copper fire engine adornments, but were nevertheless solid and reliable, performing in their hundreds throughout the London Blitz of 1940–1.

A fine study of a London fireboat crew at work, 11 July 1939. A serious fire is in progress in a warehouse just off Cannon Street, about 500yds to the right. Here, just below Cannon Street railway station, the fireboat *Massey Shaw* lays off while a land crew take a large diameter hose ashore from the fireboat's skiff to feed into pumps close by. Fireboats could pump ashore up to 8 tons of water a minute and were invaluable in Thameside firefighting operations. *Massey Shaw* went to war as part of the 'little ships' at Dunkirk only ten months later and made three successful round trips, bringing back 700 troops. Following retirement in the 1970s *Massey Shaw* was preserved and restored by a group of enthusiasts including London firefighters, and has since twice returned to the Dunkirk beaches for memorial events.

AFS recruits undergo basic hose running training supervised by a LFB sub-officer instructor (left) in preparation for war, August 1939.

An AFS knots and lines training session taken by a LFB sub-officer instructor, August 1939. Firemen were expected to be able to tie up to twenty-four different knots, in both daylight and in the dark!

The smaller AFS unit was the trailer pump, and in London 2,000 Austin taxis were 'hired' by the LFB as towing vehicles. Robust, with a small turning circle and room to carry hose and a crew, the London taxi went to war in September 1939 and proved very effective in its fire service role.

At the outbreak of war in September 1939, 23,000 volunteer auxiliaries became full-time firefighters, although until the Blitz the AFS was run as a separate organisation from the regular 'red' LFB. Here an AFS crew attached to Brompton Fire Station in west London pose for the photographer. Third from the left is former taxi driver Fred Griffiths, who was chosen by Humphrey Jennings for a lead part in the 1943 film epic *Fires Were Started*. Fred later visited the US on a government promotional tour. At the end of the war Fred went into films and television where over the next twenty-five years he played small parts in many well-known productions, right up to the *Dad's Army* series.

From their inception in 1938 the AFS suffered from a lack of suitable fire service accommodation. Many premises such as garages, workshops and even parts of school buildings were requisitioned, but generally AFS crews had to contend with spartan and makeshift arrangements. Fairly typical was AFS sub-station 37Y in Bath Street, Shoreditch, east London, seen here in June 1940.

AFS crews at Shoreditch display a wide variety of fire service 'pets', August 1940. (*Author's collection*)

Right from the start of AFS recruitment women were encouraged to enrol for general duties, including driving and communications work. However, they were given some basic firefighting training and here a squad of firewomen undergo a hose drill session, Lambeth Headquarters, June 1940.

One of the LFB's first brushes with the war came in May 1940 at the time of the Dunkirk evacuation. The Brigade was asked to provide one of its fireboats for fire cover amid the small boats fleet in Ramsgate harbour. With every boat pressed into service, the *Massey Shaw* found itself making three round trips to Dunkirk, bringing back 700 troops. Here *Massey Shaw* returns up the Thames with the fire service crew brandishing their .303 rifles, 3 June 1940.

From 7 September 1940 the Luftwaffe targeted London with day and night-time high explosive and incendiary raids, giving both regular and AFS crews their baptism of aerial raiding. Death and injury to London firemen by bombing became a regular occurrence. This hose-laying lorry was caught by a direct hit and was blown up on to the roof of a terraced house in Bonar Road, Peckham, south London, 7 September 1940. No trace of the AFS crew was ever found.

Immediately before the start of the London Blitz the Luftwaffe repeatedly raided the fuel tank installations in the Thameshaven area of Essex. London crews went in convoy to assist the overstretched local fire brigade in tackling some large and dangerous outbreaks in the fuel tanks, often under enemy fire. Below, several tanks are still burning and those nearest the camera show clear evidence of German aerial attacks, 8 September 1940.

The first phase of the London Blitz lasted for fifty-seven consecutive nights and this view shows a typical dawn scene with cooling down operations in progress. The site is Oxford Street in London's West End, with the burnt-out shell of John Lewis' department store far left, 18 September 1940.

Another early morning post-raid Blitz view looking north up Tottenham Court Road, 24 September 1940. The immense damage done to underground services is clearly shown. Firefighting quickly needed to encompass the art of relaying available water supplies from some distance away to the point of greatest need.

During the London Blitz, and raids lasting hours at a time, rapid firespread led to whole streets and blocks of buildings taking fire. With water shortages caused by shattered water mains always a difficulty, firefighters were constantly hard-pressed and in danger from falling high explosives. This is Fifty Shilling Tailors, Piccadilly, W1, on 11 October 1940.

Command and control at the scene of large London Blitz fires was always a problem. Fires involving over 1,000 firefighters at a time with 200 pumps in use were frequent, with fires covering a wide area. As mobile radio was still in its infancy, AFS dispatch riders were invaluable. Here King George VI inspects AFS dispatch riders at Lambeth Headquarters in December 1940 during the height of the Blitz.

The scene of devastation in Whitecross Street, EC1, the morning after the intense raid on the City of London, 29 December 1940. Although the raid only lasted for about four hours and involved as few as 130 German aircraft, it caused several fires which became so large as to be officially 'out of control'. In this street rapid firespread at both ends almost trapped a number of firemen and their pumps and, ordered to abandon their position, they fled to safety just in time. Ten pumps were completely burnt out as the fire engulfed the entire street.

Another view of the fire damage in Whitecross Street. At the height of this raid 1,700 LFB and AFS pumps were at work, with 300 additional pumps ordered in from brigades surrounding the London County Council LFB area. Water was at a particular premium on this night, with the nearby Thames at low tide at the height of the raid. On this night alone fourteen firemen were killed and over 250 firemen and women seriously injured during the enemy fire-raising actions.

Throughout the London Blitz many famous and historic buildings were damaged by fire. On this night of the City of London raid, 29 December 1940, St Bride, Fleet Street, one of Wren's city churches, burns fiercely. (*Daily Mirror*)

Despite the heroic efforts of fire crews, another fine building which fell to the Luftwaffe massed incendiary attack on 29 December 1940 was the banqueting hall of the Guildhall.

The famous painting by Leonard Rosoman RA is simply entitled *Wall Falling on Two Firemen, 1940*. Painted while the young artist was a serving London auxiliary fireman, this superb work dramatically captures the danger, not only of Blitz firefighting, but also of modern-day large fires. (*Imperial War Museum*)

Tabernacle Street, Shoreditch, east London, 11 January
1941. By now the Luftwaffe had been raiding London for
four months and the weary and anxious expressions on the
faces of the London firefighters were well justified.
(*Daily Mirror*)

During the Blitz 100ft turntable ladders were invaluable for
providing quick access on to roofs to deal with burning
incendiaries or to provide high level water jets. Here a
turntable ladder works to good effect in the back streets of
Shoreditch, east London, 11 January 1941.

Quite a few LFB and AFS vehicles came to grief during the Blitz raids. This Commer towing van and trailer pump have ploughed into a bomb crater just south of Southwark Bridge, 10 May 1941. Fortunately the crew escaped with minor injuries. Note the hose lines relaying water across the bridge to the north side of the river.

This night, 10 May 1941, saw the last major fire raid on London at the end of a period of virtually relentless nightly bombing. The fire service art of getting all available water from 'a' to 'b' is well illustrated, with some complicated water relays in use to boost water pressures and flow. A turntable ladder is at work at the fire on the centre right while a heavy pump and two trailer pumps feed hose lines from a portable dam. Only a few hundred yards away, to the top of this picture of Ludgate Circus, EC4, is St Paul's Cathedral, still as yet virtually undamaged.

Another fire scene on the same night, Elephant and Castle, south London. All six floors of this office block are well alight.

When Hitler's new weapon, the V1 flying bomb, first arrived in 1944, its destructive force brought new challenges for the fire service, police and other services in London. By then all fire brigades in the UK had been merged into the National Fire Service (NFS). The V1s demolished entire blocks of buildings, demanding new techniques of search and rescue to find casualties buried alive under tons of rubble. This is Middlesex Street, E1, 10 November 1944.

Many amazing V1 rescues took place. This woman is fully conscious but buried up to her neck in debris. She survived, having received only minor injuries. This photograph was taken in Manor Park, east London, on 15 November 1944.

7 THE NEW ERA

On 1 January 1948 the NFS was disbanded and control of Britain's fire brigades was returned to local authorities. Some 150 separate brigades emerged from the NFS days, with the LFB resuming its pre-war structure of sixty-one fire stations.

After the immense battering taken by the LFB during the Blitz and Flying Bomb and Rocket attacks, the early 1950s were a time of regeneration. New diesel-engined fire pumps and turntable ladders started to replace worn-out open pre-war fire engines. A new centralised '999' call handling centre was opened at Lambeth with radio links to all mobiles. By 1958 the last of London's street fire alarms had gone.

Over the past fifty years various local government reorganisations have had a profound impact upon the LFB. On 1 April 1965 the new Greater London Council took effect; this saw the LFB merging with the fire brigades of Middlesex, Croydon, East Ham, West Ham, together with some fire stations of the Essex, Kent, Surrey and Hertfordshire brigades.

Various national tragedies since the Second World War saw a number of fatal fires in factories, petrol stations, clubs, department stores, hotels and hostels. These disasters led to various new legislation where the uniformed fire service was given a primary role in the implementation and subsequent inspection of a range of fire safety measures in such premises. In addition the increase in high-rise and large building developments in the capital also saw a developing role for the Brigade's specialist fire safety teams.

Another significant aspect of the work of London's firefighters has been the steady rise in the number of 'special service' calls to non-fire emergencies. Of the total 175,000 emergency '999' calls attended by the LFB in 1999–2000 over 51,000 were to non-fire incidents such as road, rail and machinery accidents, spillages of dangerous substances, animal rescues and flooding. Nowadays London's firefighters rescue more men, women and children from life-threatening non-fire emergencies than from the old enemy. Sadly, there has also been a steady rise in the number of terrorist incidents in London; firefighters are among the first on the scene, bringing their special life-saving disciplines, skill and equipment to bear to good effect.

Further reorganisation in 1987 saw the responsibility for the LFB subsequently pass to the London Fire and Civil Defence Authority, and more recently in 2000 to the London Fire and Emergency Planning Authority (LFEPA). The LFEPA is constituted of members appointed by the London Mayor from the Greater London Authority, and from the London Boroughs and the City of London.

Much development continues to take place. In recent times all LFB firefighters have been issued with new personal protective firefighting uniforms which are as technically advanced as any in the world. Other recent replacement equipment includes pumps and aerial ladder platforms, communications and various rescue gear, together with new multi-purpose training buildings where a wide range of emergencies from live-fire scenarios to road traffic crashes can be realistically yet safely recreated.

A classic post-war fire engine shown here newly in service in London. This 1949 Dennis F7 pump escape was powered by a 150 bhp 5.7 litre Rolls-Royce engine and served initially at Lambeth Fire Station, and latterly at other fire stations in south-east London until it was retired in 1968. The F7 was a truly beautiful looking fire engine with a coach-built body and a fine road performance. Many F7s also went into service in fire brigades throughout the UK.

Three members of the Brigade were killed when the roof and upper vaults of this City warehouse suddenly crashed down into the street during a large deep-seated fire in Eldon Street, EC2, 19 November 1951. Twenty-two other firemen were seriously injured, including the Deputy Chief Fire Officer, C.P. McDuell, who lost a leg. The widespread area of the structural collapse is very evident. Each of the fire escape ladders in use on this side of the building had a crew working on them at the time of the tragedy.

Hook ladder drill *par excellence*, Lambeth Headquarters, July 1953. These co-ordinated drills during major displays started with one firemen on each side at ground floor moving up the tower to a finale with twelve firemen spectacularly hooked on to their ladder at each level. The whole drill was done to the music of *The Teddy Bears' Picnic* played by the LFB Band. There was considerable competition to get into this crack display squad.

The traditional fireman's brass pole – still the quickest method of getting a crew down into the appliance bay of a fire station and away to answer a 'shout', *c.* 1955.

Royalty were frequent visitors to see the Brigade at work and meet some of London's firefighters. Here the Duke of Edinburgh talks to a squad of new recruits during a 1957 visit to Lambeth Headquarters. Chief Fire Officer (later Sir) Freddy Delve looks on.

A view of the serious and protracted fire in the basement labyrinth off the Central Meat Markets, Smithfield, EC1, 23 January 1958. Thick choking smoke from the burning cork lining to the basement cold stores hampered firefighting efforts and it was forty hours before the fire was under control. In the early stages Station Officer Fourt-Wells and Fireman Stocking, both in breathing apparatus (BA), lost their lives when their oxygen supply ran out only feet from an exit and fresh air. This tragedy led directly to national improvements in safety devices on BA sets.

Another view of the Smithfield fire, taken thirty-six hours after the picture above, when the fire was finally extinguished. Immense damage has been caused to one end of the large market halls, but the fire was contained to the main structure despite being surrounded by other high risk premises. In all 389 pumps and 1,700 officers and men fought the fire during the forty-hour battle.

By the late 1950s the Brigade was responding to an ever increasing number of 'special service' calls – various emergencies of a non-fire nature. Typical of the steady growth in road accidents in London is this one involving an Armstrong Siddeley car in Claverton Street, Pimlico, SW1, 24 July 1958. This view shows one of the LFB breakdown lorries being used to extract the vehicle from a basement area.

A more serious special service was this accident in Tooting High Street, south London, on 10 October 1958, in which a lorry driver was trapped in his crushed cab when an insecure load of steel rods moved forward when the vehicle suddenly braked. A breakdown lorry is again in use while a London Ambulance Service Daimler waits to rush the casualty to hospital.

Many special service calls are made because of human accident and misfortune. Here a young man has fallen on to the spike of an iron railing while climbing over. Victoria Embankment, WC2, 2 September 1958.

Another road traffic accident with a breakdown lorry at work, Gloucester Street, Victoria, SW1, 19 January 1959.

Another example of the early failure of structural steel in a serious fire, followed by a total and sudden collapse of the building. Fortunately no firemen were injured in this thirty-pump blaze at the British European Airways West London Terminal, Cromwell Road, SW7, 7 December 1963.

Recruits undergo hook ladder training at Lambeth, 1964. The fireman is hooked on to the lower ladder by his special belt, enabling him to use both hands to lift the second ladder upwards to the next window, carefully guiding it with the inside of his boot. The second fireman in the team sits on the sill of the window below, out of sight. Balance, strength and confidence are all needed for there are still five more floors to go! By the end of the twelfth week of their basic course these recruits would have mastered these highly effective rescue ladders.

The aftermath of a thirty-pump fire in the historic Grocers' Hall in the heart of the City of London, 22 September 1965. Rapid firespread in a congested area presented firefighters with plenty of challenges. Here the intense fire has all but destroyed a fine oak staircase.

Another view of the Grocers' Hall, showing the damage suffered by the structure and fine fabric of the banqueting hall. At one stage firespread threatened many nearby buildings, including the Bank of England and the Mansion House. Fortunately the herculean efforts of the firefighters contained the huge fire to the Grocers' Hall complex itself.

LFB smoke eaters at work on a deep-seated fire in Great Guildford Street, Southwark, SE1, 14 January 1966. This typical 1960s view of firefighting operations, with a number of wheeled escape and turntable ladders in use, shows cooling hose lines being progressively worked into the burning warehouse off the escapes as firemen swarm up at various levels. There is little evidence of breathing apparatus in use, which at this stage would probably be being held in reserve.

One of the largest fires of the 1960s broke out in Bamburgers Timber Yard, Grovelands Road, Tottenham, N15, 22 September 1966. On a windy night fire spread in all directions, and many smaller remote fires were started by huge flying brands whipped up in the wind. Two hundred firemen with thirty pumps battled all night long amid scenes reminiscent of the Blitz.

In 1966 the Brigade celebrated 100 years of service since the formation of its forerunner, the MFB. In November the Brigade staged a Royal Review at Lambeth, attended by Her Majesty the Queen. Here, some weeks before the event, the camera captures a rehearsal of an item for the Queen's Drill Display. For this, no fewer than eight of London's twenty-nine 100ft turntable ladders came together to perform various evolutions, culminating in the breaking out of both the Union flag and that of the Brigade, high above Lambeth's drill yard.

The culmination of the Royal Review of the LFB by Her Majesty the Queen at Lambeth Headquarters in 1966 was this display of firefighting jets.

The Queen and the Duke of Edinburgh's visit continued with a tour of various parts of Headquarters. Here Chief Fire Officer Leete (left) explains the Brigade's coverage of the Greater London area in the Brigade's '999' call mobilisation centre.

For almost fifty years, up to the late 1960s, the standard LFB breathing apparatus was the Proto oxygen one-hour duration set. Although progressively improved over the years, the Proto still relied upon separate nose clips, goggles and an uncomfortable mouthpiece. Most London firemen were pleased to see the Proto replaced by compressed air sets, although oxygen sets gave a longer working duration. Here a crew from Knightsbridge Fire Station prepares to report to the breathing apparatus control point before entering the thick smoke of a fire just off Trafalgar Square, c. 1967.

Two firemen of the LFB confront the enemy, *c. 1968*.

Below: An unusual special service drama high above the streets of North Kensington, 28 January 1968. During a sudden windy squall, the jib of a tower crane at a large building site collapsed, trapping the crane operator in his cab. Crews worked for over an hour at twelfth-floor level to free him, and here firefighters prepare to ease the injured man across to the adjacent building and safety. The collapsed jib is on the right.

A major fire in a department store, Harrison Gibsons in Bromley High Street, 19 February 1968. Twenty-five pumps and three turntable ladders are involved, and this view shows different ladders at work from the constituent fire brigades which made up the enlarged Greater London Fire Brigade in 1965. Left to right: an old LFB wooden 50ft wheeled escape, a 35ft alloy ladder (ex-Kent Fire Brigade), a metal 45ft wheeled escape (ex-Croydon Fire Brigade), another ex-LFB escape and finally an ex-Kent 45ft alloy ladder.

Fires in the hostels and cheaper hotels of west London seemed to keep the LFB's 'A' Division pretty busy during the late 1960s. Here crews tackle a serious night-time bedroom fire in Queensborough Terrace, Bayswater, 23 February 1968, using a turntable ladder and several wheeled escapes. Apart from the external attack, breathing apparatus crews will be forging a path up the inside staircases through the intense heat and thick smoke to get to the burning bedroom. This was a fairly typical six-pump fire attended by about forty firefighters who were able to rescue all the hotel guests safely.

An altogether more serious outbreak occurred in the Leinster Towers Hotel, Bayswater, soon after dawn on 6 June 1969. Believed to have been started by a cigarette dropped on to bedding by a drowsy sleeper, the fire quickly took hold with smoke trapping many guests on the upper floors. The first pumps were on the scene in four minutes and quickly rescued over forty-five residents down various ladders. By the time this view was taken, about thirty minutes after the first 999 call, all rescues had been safely completed and firefighting efforts were gaining the upper hand. Note the several hook ladders in place (centre and far left).

Another view of the Leinster Towers Hotel, this time at the rear of the building. Again, hook ladders have been used to effect rescues.

The aftermath of a major accident at London's Heathrow Airport, 3 July 1968. An incoming Vanguard aircraft with a valuable cargo of racehorses returning from France crashed into two parked British European Airways Tridents. After severing the two Trident tail sections, the Vanguard collided with the terminal buildings, killing the crew and all the racehorses on board.

The LFB suffered a major tragedy on 17 July 1969. At a site known as Dudgeon's Wharf alongside the Thames in Millwall, east London, a number of large oil and fuel storage tanks were being cut up and dismantled. During this work a small fire broke out involving some residual fuel in a side tank and the Brigade was called. However, the fire had died down by the time the first crew had arrived, and while an access cover was being removed to inspect the tank interior a massive explosion took place. Five firemen and a civilian worker were killed instantly. This picture is of the full Brigade funeral a week later and shows the arrival of the first coffins for the memorial service. Apart from several thousand London firefighters, the funeral service was attended by firefighters from virtually every other UK brigade.

Another London fire tragedy, Crawford Street, W1, 14 October 1969. An elderly couple died amid the thick smoke on the third floor in this tenement block fire, which was caused by a defective electrical heater. Although the fire is now out, the massed ladders indicate the initial concerted effort to get into the front of the flat to try and save the couple.

On 10 November 1969 high winds caused tons of scaffolding to crash down into Whitehall Place, partly crushing a foreign embassy car parked below. Both the diplomat and his driver were trapped, and, although they were both cut free, they subsequently died from their injuries.

A view which captures typical London firefighting operations in the late 1960s. There has been a small, yet severe, bedroom fire above a bookmaker's in the East End, December 1969. The fire has become a four pumper. Here crews work off a wheeled escape (left) and an extension ladder to provide hose lines into the upper floors, where breathing apparatus crews are extinguishing the fire.

Another four pumper, this time in a food store in Fulham Road, Fulham, west London, January 1970. The shop window has shattered because of the build-up of heat, and BA crews are deep inside the hot, black smoke, seeking out the seat of the fire. Extra BA wearers in Proto sets prepare to descend into the basement. (*Tony Jafrato*)

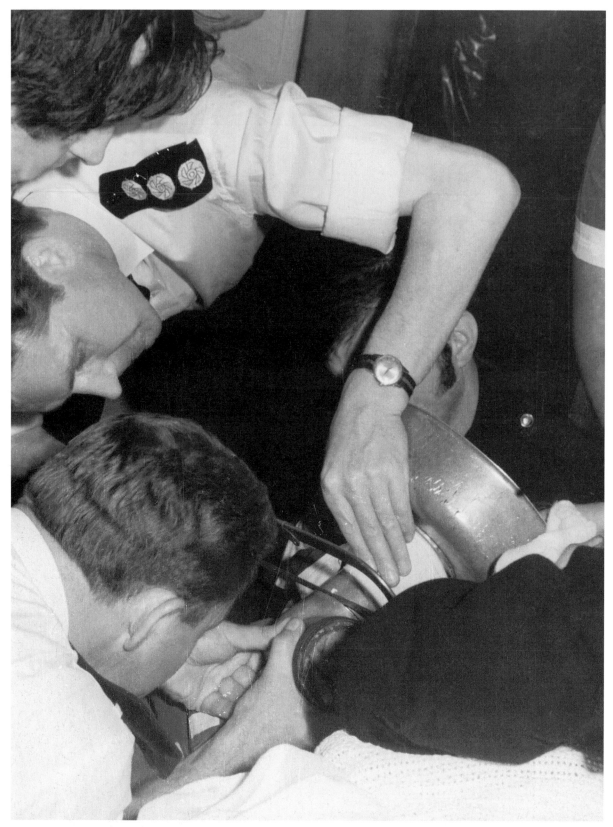

This special service rescue came about after a young boy stuck his fingers in a mincing machine in his father's shop. This view shows fire crews, in conjunction with a medical team, carefully cutting off the outer metal shell of the mincer in the Accident and Emergency Department of St Mary's Hospital, Praed Street, Paddington, W2, before doctors tried to save the boy's hand, 12 June 1970.

This rather artistic study captures three London firefighters wearing anti-flash gear as they deal with a fire involving some oxygen and other types of cylinders in a workshop off Kilburn High Road, March 1970.

The light from this fire in a furniture factory, Essex Road, Islington, April 1971, reflects on the helmet of the fireman as he directs a powerful water jet into the flames. (*Joe Bulaitis*)

By 1970 few large Victorian Thameside warehouses were left intact as the old dockside area started to be redeveloped. However, several major fires did break out in those that remained. The fire in this empty five-floor building in Wapping High Street, May 1971, was caused by vagrants who were sleeping rough in the premises. It developed into a twenty-pump affair, reminiscent of the great fires of Victorian times.

Below: Another, even larger, riverside warehouse fire took place on 9 August 1971, in Battlebridge Lane, off Tooley Street, SE1, very close to the site of the huge fire which killed James Braidwood 110 years before. The six-floor warehouse was a cold store, lined with cork and other insulating material, and the fire burned for seven hours before 200 London firefighters, using forty pumps, gained control. Thick smoke hung over the river and across to the City throughout the day, blocking out the summer sun. Note Tower Bridge in the middle distance and the fireboat alongside (left) providing firefighting water from the Thames.

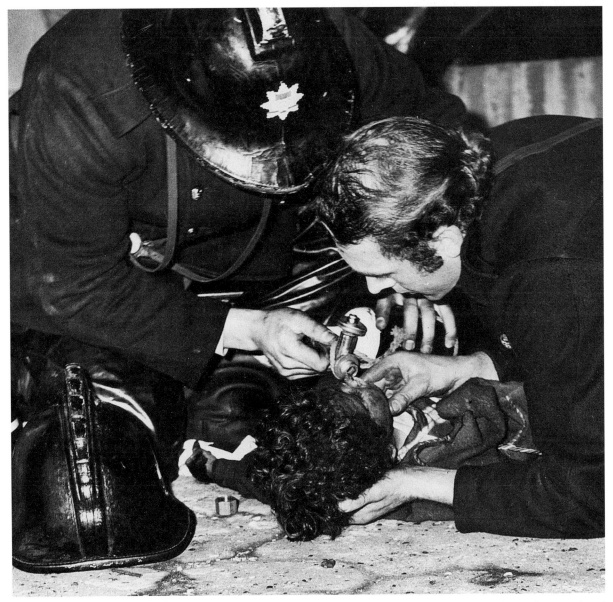

Two London firefighters fight desperately to resuscitate a young child overcome by smoke after being rescued from a fire in residential flats in the Elephant and Castle, south London, 10 December 1971. (*Owen Rowlands*)

This scene could be from the London Blitz but it is, in fact, lunchtime on 22 May 1972. Very rapid firespread has soon engulfed this shop and office block at Gardiner's Corner, Whitechapel, east London, and crews are putting up a water curtain to protect the premises (left) threatened by the intense radiated heat.

Only ten minutes after the first 999 call to Gardiner's Corner, Whitechapel, another 100ft turntable ladder (from Barbican Fire Station) is quickly positioned in response to urgent requests for the assistance of more pumps and firefighters.

Pictured in 1972, this Dennis emergency tender (ET), based at Finchley in north London, was one of eight serving the Brigade's area. Virtually travelling workshops, carrying a wide range of specialist rescue gear, these ETs responded to road and rail accidents and to all manner of humanitarian emergencies. ETs also attended large fires where their experienced crews and considerable breathing apparatus capability were invaluable.

In 1972 the Brigade ran four Dennis hose-laying lorries, each capable of running out up to a mile of large capacity hose at 30 mph at serious London fires where water supplies were poor. This is Hendon's hose-laying lorry showing the method of stowing flaked hose. Note the well-tended forecourt border on the right.

Four views of firefighting operations following the fire caused by an IRA incendiary device in Westminster Hall on 17 June 1974. Above, some of the first firefighters on the scene are making an aerial attack on the fire in support of the breathing apparatus crews at work inside the historic building.

This view shows a crew at work using hook ladders to remove a number of large, heavy slates to ensure that all the fire is out inside the roof structure.

Another view of firefighters at work on the roof of Westminster Hall. By now a large section of slates has been removed, the fire is fully extinguished and the incident under control.

The general scene on one flank outside Westminster Hall during the latter stages of firefighting operations. In the foreground an emergency stand-by breathing apparatus crew is ready while a 100ft turntable ladder (far left), a 50ft wheeled escape and an extension ladder are all in use.

The Worsley Hotel fire in Maida Vale, W9, on Friday 13 December 1974 came to epitomise every challenge ever likely to face a firefighter. In the early hours 200 London firemen tackled two separate fires lit by an arsonist which trapped thirty-six residents at windows on upper floors. All were rescued safely, although six people died inside the inferno. About one hour after the first call, part of the hotel's upper floors suddenly collapsed, trapping a team of four firemen beneath tons of burning debris. Here the protracted rescue of fireman by fireman is under way. The trapped crew are inside the room top right and two turntable ladders are ready above, if needed.

After ninety minutes of careful digging and extrication the first firefighter, Tony Stewart, was released. Soon after Station Officer Colin Searl was freed, and here he is carried to a waiting ambulance. His eyes tell of the hell he has been through. The third casualty, Fireman Martin Walker, was released about an hour later. All three were badly burnt but survived. Sadly, the last member of the crew, Fireman Hamish Pettit, died in the collapse. The Queen subsequently awarded eight gallantry medals to firemen who served at this fire, the largest number ever given for a single peacetime UK incident. One of these went posthumously to Fireman Pettit.

The Worsley Hotel fire well illustrated the dangers of firefighting in Victorian and Edwardian buildings, with their vulnerable stone staircases. Exposed to severe fire, they can suddenly collapse, as happened here. Note the widespread fire damage as fire has swept up the staircase as if it were a chimney.

The value of properly installed and maintained self-closing fire resisting doors was evident after the Worsley fire. This door was one of a number which stopped lateral spread of fire into adjacent hotel blocks. The building fabric on the other side of the door is virtually undamaged.

An unusual rescue involved a steeplejack who became ill while at the top of a chimney in Woolwich, south-east London, 18 May 1974. A firefighter scaled the chimney and stayed with the casualty until they were lifted off by Royal Navy helicopter.

When a rush hour Northern Line Underground train ran through Moorgate station and crashed at speed into a dead end tunnel, the LFB were called upon to mount one of its biggest ever rescue operations. Forty-two passengers were killed but many more were trapped in the crumpled carriages inside the tunnel. The last live casualty was freed after some twelve hours, but the recovery of bodies took a further five days and nights and involved 1,000 firefighters working in short shifts because of the heat and fetid condition deep into the tunnel. Here crews wriggle past the rear carriages to get to the worst part of the crash, 28 February 1975.

A view of extrication operations about twenty hours after the Moorgate crash, 1 March 1975.

After all the live Moorgate casualties had been extracted, crews were able to begin the grim task of releasing those killed in the crash. By then, all rescue teams were forced to wear breathing apparatus because of the deteriorating air quality in the deep dead-end tunnel of death.

Turnout, and the adrenaline flows: a scene from the late 1970s as Harrow Fire Station's pump escape and pump respond to yet another 999 call.

A considerable test of the Brigade's capability came on 31 March 1986, when fire broke out in a residence within Hampton Court Palace, south-west London. The fire glow can be seen at rooftop level as reinforcing crews get to work in support of firefighters already up on the roof. Twenty pumps attended but the fire was contained without major damage to the main structure of the Palace.

Here, as the charred debris begins to cool down, the Brigade's specialist forensic officers begin the task of establishing just how and where the Hampton Court fire started.

Extensive damage was caused when a gas explosion partly demolished this block of residential flats in Putney Hill, south-west London, January 1985. Several residents were buried and newly acquired thermal imaging cameras were used to help locate their whereabouts.

A successful animal rescue, 21 March 1987. This dog was affected by smoke when a public house caught fire. Here the fire is under control and the sub-officer is about to hand the dog over to the RSPCA, none too much the worse for his experience.

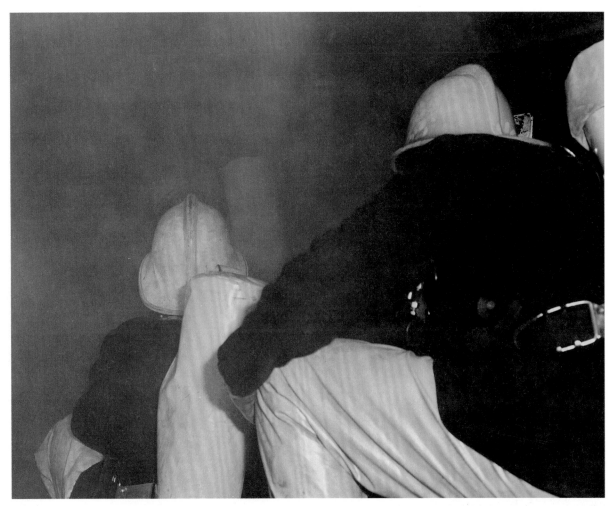

Following the flashover and fireball which engulfed a Piccadilly Line escalator at King's Cross Underground Station on 18 November 1987, fire crews in breathing apparatus work their way into the intense heat and smoke as they descend into the awful physical conditions during the early stages of rescue and firefighting operations.

Another view of the King's Cross fire, taken at one of the many fire-scarred entrances looking down into the booking hall. Here breathing apparatus crews take a brief break and anxiously look for reinforcements to search the labyrinth of underground passageways in which many passengers are believed still trapped by smoke.

The doomed Piccadilly Line escalator at Kings Cross, showing the severity of the fire damage. It was here and in the nearby booking hall that most of the thirty victims died, along with Station Officer Colin Townsley, as he tried to save them.

A view showing the horrific fire damage at the top of the fatal King's Cross escalator. The subsequent public inquiry led to a no smoking policy on Underground stations, and better protective uniforms and tighter procedures for the LFB.

A fond farewell to a gallant hero. Crews from Soho Fire Station carry the body of their station officer, Colin Townsley, in traditional style on their 'chariot of fire' to Lewisham Crematorium on 27 November 1987. Traffic came to a standstill in central London and many onlookers were in tears as the cortège passed. Fire officers from all over Britain and abroad lined the final approach to the crematorium, and wreaths included one in the shape of a white helmet and another in letters spelling 'GUV'. Townsley was later posthumously awarded the George Medal for gallantry.

Another view of Colin Townsley's funeral cortège, 27 November 1987. (*The Independent*)

Prime Minister Mrs Thatcher visited the scene of the King's Cross fire disaster some hours after the incident was under control. 'I was shaken and horrified by the disaster,' she said. 'What you don't get a feeling of, except by being with the firemen, is the intense heat in a limited space – they lived up to the best British tradition.' (*Press Association*)

Thirty-five passengers lost their lives when three rush hour trains collided just outside Clapham Junction, 12 December 1988. The rescue of seventy seriously injured casualties and dealing with the major outbreak was a huge teamwork operation involving the LFB, the Metropolitan Police, the London Ambulance Service and mobile medical hospital teams.

Another view of the Clapham Junction crash site, 12 December 1988.
(*Press Association*)

On 4 March 1989, barely three months after the Clapham train crash, the Brigade was faced with another major rescue task when five people died and more than eighty were injured when two trains collided near Purley station, only 9 miles from the scene of the Clapham Junction disaster. Seven carriages overturned, plunging down a steep embankment and narrowly missing houses.

Special services come in an increasing variety of challenges for the Brigade. Here a train on the Docklands Light Railway has overshot the buffer stops and hangs precariously in mid-air. Fortunately no serious injuries occurred.

One of London's best-loved theatres was badly damaged by fire and collapse on 12 February 1990. The fire at the Savoy Theatre, located behind the famous hotel in the Strand, was tackled by crews from a wide area of central, north and south London. Sadly, although the blaze was under control in just over two hours, much of the theatre's celebrated art deco interior had been destroyed.

In more recent years London's firefighters have occasionally got caught up in civil unrest in the capital. Here, during the poll tax riots, on 31 March 1990, ten pumps deal with a fire caused by an arsonist in a building under reconstruction in Trafalgar Square.

A very unusual animal incident took place in the Thames on 22 May 1990 when the crew of the London fireboat *London Phoenix* noticed a dolphin in distress near Vauxhall Bridge. The firefighters managed to get the dolphin into shallow water and call specialist help but, sadly, the dolphin died.

Following the Royal tradition of interest in the LFB, Prince Harry eagerly takes the wheel of this 1936 Leyland Metz turntable ladder after he, his mother, the Princess of Wales, and Prince William attended a service to commemorate the fiftieth anniversary of the London Blitz, 25 October 1990.

The third serious train crash inside a two-year period occurred on 8 January 1991 when an inbound rush hour commuter train ran into the buffer stops at Cannon Street. Two passengers died and many were trapped inside the crumpled front carriages. Here the extraction and rescue operation involving fire and medical teams is well under way.

Special services come in all shapes and sizes. Here passengers are assisted down from a Central Line Underground train in mid-tunnel between stations following a disruption caused by a major power failure, 19 February 1991.

On 4 May 1991 outside St Paul's Cathedral Her Majesty Queen Elizabeth the Queen Mother unveiled a memorial to the firefighters of British fire brigades who lost their lives in the air raids of the Second World War.

A particularly difficult firefighting task faced crews at this serious fire in a modern office complex in Minster Court, Mark Lane, EC1, in the City of London, 7 August 1991. The firefighting operation to extinguish the fire in the roof space ten floors up required the co-ordinated efforts of 100 firefighters and twenty pumps plus a number of aerial ladders.

At the other end of the firefighting scale, this severe fire and explosion in a terrace house in St John's Wood, NW8, on 23 November 1991 is being tackled by a four-pump attendance (about twenty firefighters). Several breathing apparatus teams are up in the first floor and inside the roof space.

A partly extended 100ft turntable ladder at work above a large fire in a warehouse complex, Deptford, 4 February 1992.

A splendid view of the roof of the Palace of Westminster looking towards Big Ben, 13 March 1992. Two firefighters take a breather after four crews had dealt with a fire in a tank room situated closely above the Commons chamber. The fire was caused when contractors' hot work ignited dust and pipework lagging in the tank room. Here the firefighter on the right is using a thermal imaging camera to assess the condition of the contractor's acetylene cylinder which became involved in the fire and was removed and immersed in a cooling dam rigged up by the Brigade on the roof. The fire was unique in parliamentary history as it created the first occasion when the business of the House of Commons was interrupted by a 'fire' evacuation.

Sadly, in more recent years the work of the LFB has had to embrace the aftermath of terrorist activities. Here, in a scene reminiscent of the London Blitz, firefighters are making buildings safe after the huge bomb blast in St Mary Axe, EC3, in the City of London, 10 April 1992. The gas main in the foreground is allowed to burn under controlled conditions. Three city workers died in the explosion.

Another view, taken the morning after, showing the huge scale of the damage around the area of the St Mary Axe bombing.

When the heavens opened over north London one morning there was widespread flash flooding. Fifty firefighters and ten pumps were at work here in Tollington Road, Holloway, N7, on 15 October 1992.

Arson is a growing problem throughout the United Kingdom and churches are particularly vulnerable. This view shows the sad aftermath of an eight-pump fire in Calton Avenue, North Dulwich, SE21, on 7 December 1992.

Terrorists returned to the City of London on 24 August 1993 when a huge bomb in Bishopsgate, EC2, caused considerable damage over a wide area. Twenty pumps and 100 firefighters were involved in initial rescues of many injured people, and subsequently in the massive safety and clear up operation.

The Queen Mother once again showed an interest in the LFB when on 6 July 1993 she visited Southgate Fire Station in north London, following the success of firefighters based there in winning a section in the London Gardens Competition.

Firefighting and medical teams bring all their combined skills and experience to bear as they work to release a seriously injured driver whose car has collided with a tree in Lewisham, south-east London, on 10 July 1993.

This lorry has come to grief on its side perched high up on a slip road off the North Circular Road at Waterworks Corner, Tottenham, 20 July 1993. The driver was trapped in his cab and his rescue took three hours. Note the aerial ladder platform (ALP) providing a working base for firefighters, a pump ladder parked to protect the ALP and a rescue unit providing support on the other side of the crash site.

Another serious and tragic fire, this time at St John's Church, Cator Road, Sydenham, south London, 11 September 1993.

On 20 January 1994 firefighters were unable to enter this blazing nine-storey flour silo in Canning Town, east London, E16, because of its unsafe condition and danger of imminent collapse. Eight crews brought the fire under control in just over two hours and limited the damage to the building itself.

Even London firefighters occasionally rescue other animals than cats up trees! On 12 February 1994 this bull was dug out of the mud by crews from Sidcup Fire Station, south-east London, who then used slings and a hydraulic platform to haul him to safety and the care of a vet.

On the occasion of a visit by the Duchess of Kent to the Brigade's Training Centre at Southwark, 29 March 1994, the camera captures Her Royal Highness apparently being reassured by instructor Station Officer John Moriarty that a ride up in an aerial platform is really quite safe!

A view of some of the LFB's logistical support necessary for modern day firefighting. This mobile unit is one of a number of strategically situated units which is put in place at serious fires to provide breathing apparatus crews with full servicing facilities.

Working from an upwind position, two London firefighters feel the heat as they get to grips with a fire in a tyre dump which is producing plenty of thick toxic smoke, 4 September 1995.

Over recent years the Brigade has developed fire investigation teams to look at certain causes of fires immediately after the blaze is extinguished. This fire has been caused by a smoker's cigarette being dropped into his bedding after he fell asleep. Careless disposal of cigarettes and smoking materials is still a major cause of fire.

Another high incidence cause of fires is unattended cooking. The aftermath of this deep fat fryer left on an electric hob is all too obvious. With the attention of the cook distracted, the oil in the fryer has eventually ignited and the fire quickly spread to engulf the entire kitchen.

When a contractor's tar boiler caught fire on the roof of one of the capital's tallest buildings, the NatWest Tower in the City, in mid-afternoon on 17 January 1996, the smoke from the top of this prominent structure quickly led to over 500 separate '999' fire calls being received at London Fire Brigade Control. The crews of six pumps had to be deployed to get up the forty-five floors of the tower and extinguish the fire, even though this was a relatively minor outbreak.

The driver of this passing van had a shock when an executive jet skidded and ran off the runway at Northolt Airport and crashed on to the busy A40 Western Avenue, 13 August 1996. Fortunately there was no fire or serious injury. Although the incident is now under control, a Defence Fire Services (DFS) foam tender stands guard in the background while LFB and DFS crews begin to sort out their equipment. Note the protective foam carpet laid around the scene.

A dramatic night time scene at the height of a major fire in a block of flats under refurbishment at Selsdon Court, Southall, west London, 15 November 1996.

Not a great fire, but nevertheless one that gives a general idea of the potential problems of tunnel firefighting under London. During the construction of the Heathrow Express link into the airport, this constructor's rail trolley caught fire at Sipson Lane, 2 December 1996. Note the blackened concrete above and beyond caused by what has been a fairly small outbreak.

The buildings involved in this fire at a west London warehouse on 3 December 1996 quickly became too unsafe for firefighters to work inside. Here the turntable ladder (right) and an aerial ladder platform (left) project powerful water jets into the heart of the fire.

Another, closer, view of an aerial ladder platform at work, showing the operator carefully bringing the cage slowly into the first-floor window in support of the firefighting crews working in breathing apparatus inside, 1 January 1997.

Bexley High Street, south-east London, 4 February 1997: following the derailment of a freight train which demolished several buildings adjacent to the railway, it was feared that several persons might be trapped under the debris. Here a firefighter uses a sound detector unit to check the affected area. Fortunately no buried casualties were found.

Gas cylinders involved in fire pose particular hazards for firefighters. This gas cylinder became overheated in a laboratory fire and suddenly exploded with violent force. These flying jagged metal pieces are lethal, apart from the added danger from flammable or toxic cylinder contents.

Fire in London's new Dockland, 12 April 1997. Here, alongside the London Arena building and close by Canary Wharf (left centre), fire has started in a floating restaurant. The crews of four pumps are already at work (right) while the LFB fireboat *London Phoenix* comes alongside in close support.

Two views of the same fire which started in a car breaker's yard in Grosvenor Terrace, Camberwell, SE5, 18 May 1997. The overall scene above shows the fire spreading fast in all directions into surrounding buildings. Already aerial firefighting jets are at work on two faces of the fire in a containment exercise.

The other edge of the same fireground scene. Fire has now spread into an unoccupied chapel and is threatening the flats above the shops on the left. Fifteen pumps and seventy-five firefighters successfully got the upper hand after three hours of hard effort.

Firefighters nationally are increasingly called upon to deal with hazardous materials. Apart from understanding how substances that can be highly dangerous might react to fire and spillage, firefighters also need to protect themselves from contact with these hazardous materials. Here, an LFB training session is underway with two firefighters rigged out in all enclosing chemical protection suits. The two men are wearing breathing apparatus *inside* the suits and both must be sweltering on this sunny afternoon, 13 May 1997.

Nowadays all '999' calls to the LFB are handled at the Command and Mobilisation Centre at Lambeth Headquarters. In addition to taking and dealing with emergency calls, control personnel also arrange back-up resources for lengthy incidents. They also mobilise specialist support such as petroleum and hazardous materials officers and the fire investigation teams, and constantly monitor the availability of London's 113 fire stations covering the 620 square miles of Greater London.

Apart from its statutory role which includes enforcing fire safety in hotels, offices and factories, and advising local authorities on licensed premises, the Brigade also puts a great effort into community and school fire safety campaigns. Here Brixton Fire Station Commander Roy George advises a local resident on how to fix her family's smoke alarm during National Fire Safety Week, on 30 September 1997.

Another horrendous train crash that challenged the rescue abilities of the Brigade occurred at Southall, west London, on 19 September 1997. A London-bound Intercity train collided with a freight train, resulting in six fatalities and twenty-five passengers trapped in the front part of the train. Here extrication of those trapped is well under way.

An unusual special service took place on 27 October 1997 at the Thames Barrier when the MV *Sand Kite* collided with the lock gates. This view is taken from the fireboat *London Phoenix*, which stood by until all the stricken vessel's crew were safely taken off.

This Class 86 Intercity electric locomotive was in sidings at Willesden, north London, when fire broke out in an electrical compartment, 4 December 1997. Here a breathing apparatus crew carefully negotiate the cramped interior of the locomotive to deal with the burning cables.

On 12 December 1997 a fire broke out in a fast food bar in Terminal One at Heathrow Airport. The fire quickly spread through service ducting into the roof, causing some severe damage, but was contained after about an hour. By that time crews had successfully cut off the risk of firespread into the huge complex. The sheer physical task of running hose lines out to protect the terminal is well shown in this view, which was taken as crews were clearing up. The fire virtually shut down Heathrow operations for several hours and delays to travellers were extensive.

This spectacular fire occurred in a flat on the twelfth floor of Chillingford House, Blackshaw Road, Tooting, SW17, 5 March 1998. Six pumps tackled the outbreak using the inbuilt firefighting features incorporated in all of London's high-rise buildings. Note the prodigious amount of thick smoke being produced.

A roof fire has been successfully extinguished by fifty firefighters in this fine terraced City building in Minster Court, Mincing Lane, EC3, 24 March 1998. Here clearing up operations are in progress and an aerial ladder platform still provides access to the roof.

Athough this arson fire on 23 April 1998 involved only a few wooden cable drums and a quantity of rubbish stored deep under the A40 Westway in Harrow Road, Paddington, it did threaten adjoining premises. Fifty firefighters had to penetrate a considerable distance into the swirling smoke and intense heat to locate and extinguish the fire.

In 1998 the LFB adopted a completely new firefighting rig for all its 6,000 operational firefighters. The final design of the firefighters' protection had been decided after a lengthy trial of many types of apparel. Here three firefighters show off their new twenty-first-century rig, 23 June 1998.

At the time of the introduction of the new rig the Brigade took the opportunity to parade firefighters wearing various uniforms dating back over the last 133 years. Here are (right to left): MFB 1866, LFB 1935–41, National Fire Service 1941–8, LFB 1950, 1973, 1985 and 1998.

A turntable ladder operator's view of a serious fire in a top-floor flat in Courtfield Gardens, Earls Court, SW5, 8 January 1999. The fire is now out and breathing apparatus crews are beginning to ventilate the building. Note the range of operations indicator quadrant to the right of the operator, whose skill in positioning the ladder when fully extended to 100ft is critical to safe rescue and firefighting operations at upper levels. The fire was caused by a candle.

Another view of a turntable ladder at work during an eight-pump fire in a building undergoing refurbishment in Old Park Lane, W1, 31 January 1999.

A famous media face dons a London firefighter's uniform, 2 May 1999. Richard Branson looks intent as fire crews bring a serious fire in his London offices in Holland Park, W11, under control. He had borrowed the rig to enter his building (guided by an LFB officer) after the fire was under control.

An aerial view of a rapidly spreading fire in an open plan school, Woolwich, SE18, 3 May 1999. Firefighters have their work cut out to prevent the flames travelling to remote parts of the building through false ceilings and service ducts. Twenty-three separate '999' calls were received to the incident, which required twelve pumps and a total force of seventy firefighters.

Regular training ensures that London firefighters are always ready for action, whatever the operational challenge. Intensive drill sessions are staged daily, during which all manner of imaginary fire and rescue incidents are masochistically created. Here, under the watchful eye of Croydon Fire Station Commander (right), several crews get to work into a training building using hose lines, ladders and breathing apparatus, 19 May 1999.

Breathing apparatus (BA) is virtually a firefighter's personal life support system amid the toxic smoke given off by modern plastic materials. This crew from West Norwood Fire Station prepare to enter the Brigade's BA training complex at Croydon to carry out a 'search' mission, 19 May 1999. Note the sub-officer (right) who is responsible for the safety of BA wearers inside.

One of the Brigade's newer training buildings is located at the Southwark Training Centre. Here a combined pump and ladder drill involving crews from several fire stations is in progress, 21 May 1999.

Command and Control at a serious incident is always critical towards operational success. To provide this, the Brigade has a number of mobile local control units for medium sized fires and special services, but for major events the Headquarters' Control Unit responds from Lambeth. Here the impressive Headquarters Control Unit poses outside the Palace of Westminster.

In 1999 the Brigade commissioned two new fireboats, *Firedart* and *Fireflash*, and here they pause on the Thames with the Millennium Dome as a backdrop, 27 July 1999.

The sheer force of a gas explosion followed by a fire is shown in the devastation caused to this semi-detached house, Redlands Way, Brixton, SW2, 6 July 1999. A LFB crew carefully check through the debris.

During the rush hour of 6 October 1999 two trains collided head-on at Ladbroke Grove, North Kensington, W10, trapping many passengers in the wreckage. Fire also broke out. The Brigade mounted a massive rescue operation in conjunction with police and medical services. This view shows the extent of the wreckage strewn across the crash site.

Another view of the impacted wreckage of the two trains. Despite the fatal casualties, many successful rescues were carried out.

Following the Ladbroke Grove disaster, Her Majesty the Queen paid a brief visit to Lambeth Headquarters to meet personally some of the rescue teams involved in the crash. Here, the Queen, accompanied by Deputy Chief Fire Officer Roy Bishop (left), talks to some of the crews. (*PA News*)

Similarly, Home Secretary Jack Straw also visited Lambeth to recognise the outstanding work of the LFB during the Ladbroke Grove tragedy. Here, London's Chief Fire Officer Brian Robinson chats with some of his firefighters before they meet the Home Secretary.

Following a spillage of toxic chemicals in south London on 4 March 2000, firefighters are required to undergo a standard decontamination process before getting out of their protective suits and breathing apparatus sets.

One aspect of the Brigade's recent domestic fire safety campaign is aimed at reducing chip pan fires. Here, during a demonstration in a shopping centre on 13 May 2000, a firefighter has allowed a heated chip pan to ignite whilst left on a stove. He then shows the dangerous effect of pouring water on to the fire, instead of using a fire blanket once the heat source is turned off.

In February 2001 the Brigade commissioned the operational use of a dog for fire investigation purposes, and in so doing recalled the presence of fire dogs in the LFEE back in the 1830s. The new recruit was Odin, a nineteen-month-old Labrador. Working alongside the Brigade's Fire Investigation Teams, his role is as a 'sniffer' dog in tracing accelerants used in suspicious fires. A dog's sense of smell is 200 times more sensitive than that of a human and Odin has already been successful in his new role. Here he poses with his handler, Station Officer Pat Lyon, at their New Cross, south-east London base, 11 September 2000.

As the Palace of Westminster has suffered some major fires, not least in 1834 when most of the then Palace was totally destroyed, the authorities of both Houses take fire very seriously. Recognising that the LFB will have a difficult task when trying to locate and deal with a fire in the tortuous interior of the Palace, regular familiarisation visits take place. The Brigade also stages periodic exercises, liaising closely with the Palace's own Fire Section, all of whom are ex-LFB personnel. This view shows a 1993 exercise in progress involving six pumps and other specialist vehicles. (*Philip Wright, Serjeant at Arms*)

A key part of the firefighting strategy at the Palace of Westminster is the use of a fireboat on the Thames frontage to provide copious supplies of water from the river. Here the fireboat *London Phoenix* lies off the Palace terrace with two lines of hose already ashore. (*Philip Wright, Serjeant at Arms*)

This view of LFB pumps easing their way through an archway into an inner courtyard demonstrates the difficulty of ready access for firefighting teams into many of London's historic buildings. (*Philip Wright, Serjeant at Arms*)

The workhorse fire engine of the LFB fleet is the Pump Ladder. Normally crewed by between four or six firefighters, this Volvo carries 300 gallons of water, 1,400ft of hose, 45 and 30ft extension ladders, breathing apparatus, and cutting and lifting equipment.

These Volvo Fire Rescue Units attend all major fires and crashes, building collapses, chemical incidents and underground emergencies. They carry a wide range of powerful rescue tools and other specialist equipment.

The radiated heat can almost be felt in this spectacular view of a large fire in a warehouse and offices in Bath Street, EC1, 7 September 1998.

An unusual modern-day view of firefighters based at the LFB headquarters at Lambeth, 16 June 1999. On the right is their Pump Ladder, while on the left is the Brigade Command Unit.

Flooding again affects the London area, and here fire crews from Hayes, west London, come to the aid of a grateful public. (*Hounslow Chronicle*)

How did that get up there? A pet boa constrictor snake has escaped from safe keeping and has somehow got up on the roof of the house. His owner looks apprehensive as a firefighter carefully eases the unusual pet down to safety.

A timeless image of a firefighter at work, here removing glass from a window frame during clearing-up and salvage operations. (*PA News*)

A view of the LFB crews at work, dramatically highlighted by the fire glow.

During the late 1990s the LFB became one of the first UK brigades to conduct an extensive trial into the use of a helicopter response to particular life-threatening incidents such as road crashes and similar urgent humanitarian rescue emergencies. However, despite being able to beat traffic delays and rapidly get crews to an emergency site, the considerable costs of maintaining helicopter cover for fire service use has to be set against other financial demands. As yet no UK fire brigade has a dedicated helicopter facility, although the LFB continues to work closely with the Metropolitan Police Aerial Branch. Here, during the period of the LFB trial, the Brigade helicopter keeps close company over the City of London with the Metropolitan Police and a London Air Ambulance aircraft. (*Marcus Taylor*)

Part of the fine carvings on the Memorial and Roll of Honour at Lambeth Headquarters.

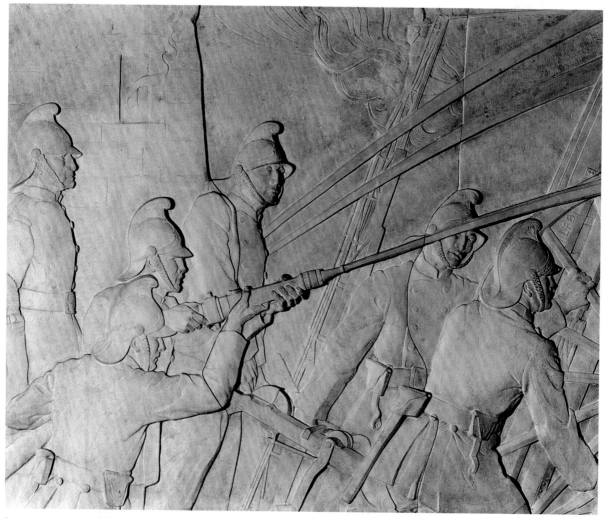

In memoriam. Part of the impressive memorial at Lambeth Headquarters to the men and women of the LFB who have died in the line of duty.

LONDON'S FIRE SERVICE IN 2001

The London Fire Brigade badge was used from the coming of the Greater London Council in 1965 until 2000, when the badge was redesigned upon the inception of the Greater London Authority.

Today's London Fire Brigade is one of the largest fire brigades in the world. Its 5,900 firefighters and officers based at London's 112 land fire stations and one river station protect people and property from fire and other hazards within the 620 square miles of Greater London. Among London's uniformed firefighters are 300 members drawn from the ethnic community and seventy female firefighters. About 1,300 non-uniformed staff are also employed in various support roles across the Brigade's operational area.

In 1999–2000 the LFB attended over 175,000 '999' calls. Each of these was received at the Brigade's high-tech Command and Mobilising Centre at Lambeth HQ, who mobilise the nearest firefighting resources to the scene of each callout. All emergencies are responded to immediately, however great or small, and within the governmental time targets for getting to fires.

Within the uniformed force are specialist officers whose specific role is to enforce fire safety law, to offer advice on general fire safety matters, and to reduce the risk of fire occurring. The main causes of accidental fire in London are:

Misuse of cooking and domestic appliances	65%
Faulty electrical appliances and wiring faults	15%
Smoking materials including naked flame	10%
Other (such as clothes too close to heaters)	9%
Unknown	1%

It is a fact that 81 per cent of all fires in the home are accidental and 19 per cent are caused deliberately. In addition, those particularly at risk are elderly persons, young children and those who live in areas of social and economic deprivation.

In 2000 the Brigade launched a community fire safety programme in which local firefighters spend more time working directly with their local community promoting fire safety. The target is to reduce all fire deaths in London by 20 per cent and to reduce fires in total by 20 per cent over a five-year period, from 2000 to 2005.

LONDON FIRE BRIGADE
FIRE STATION LOCATIONS

Southern

Boroughs
Bexley, Bromley, Croydon, Greenwich, Kingston-upon-Thames, Lambeth, Lewisham, Merton, Southwark, Sutton, Wandsworth.

Fire Stations
Addington, Battersea, Beckenham, Bexley, Biggin Hill, Brixton, Bromley, Clapham, Croydon, Deptford, Dockhead, Downham, East Greenwich, Eltham, Erith, Forest Hill, Greenwich, Kingston, Lambeth, Lambeth (River), Lee Green, Lewisham, Mitcham, New Cross, New Malden, Norbury, Old Kent Road, Orpington, Peckham, Plumstead, Purley, Sidcup, Southwark, Surbiton, Sutton, Tooting, Wallington, Wandsworth, West Norwood, Wimbledon, Woodside, Woolwich.

Eastern

Boroughs
Barking and Dagenham, City of London, Enfield, Hackney, Haringey, Havering, Islington, Newham, Redbridge, Tower Hamlets, Waltham Forest.

Fire Stations
Barking, Bethnal Green, Bow, Chingford, Clerkenwell, Dagenham, Dowgate, East Ham, Edmonton, Enfield, Hainault, Holloway, Homerton, Hornchurch, Hornsey, Ilford, Islington, Kingsland, Leyton, Leytonstone, Millwall, Plaistow, Poplar, Romford, Shadwell, Shoreditch, Silvertown, Southgate, Stoke Newington, Stratford, Tottenham, Walthamstow, Wennington, Whitechapel, Woodford.

Western

Boroughs
Barnet, Brent, Camden, Ealing, Harrow, Hillingdon, Hammersmith and Fulham, Hounslow, Kensington and Chelsea, Richmond upon Thames, Westminster.

Fire Stations
Acton, Barnet, Belsize, Chelsea, Chiswick, Ealing, Euston, Feltham, Finchley, Fulham, Hammersmith, Harrow, Hayes, Heathrow, Hendon, Heston, Hillingdon, Kensington, Kentish Town, Knightsbridge, Manchester Square, Mill Hill, Northolt, North Kensington, Paddington, Park Royal, Richmond, Ruislip, Soho, Southall, Stanmore, Twickenham, Wembley, West Hampstead, Westminster, Willesden.

FURTHER READING

Fire and Water – A National Fire Service Anthology, Lindsay Drummond, 1942

Firebrace, Sir Aylmer, *Fire Service Memories*, Andrew Melrose, 1948

Henham, Brian, *True Hero: The Life and Times of James Braidwood*, Brian Henham, 2000

Holloway, Sally, *London's Noble Fire Brigades*, Cassell, 1973

Holloway, Sally, *Courage High*, HMSO, 1992

Holloway, Sally and Wallington, Neil, *Fire and Rescue*, Patrick Stephens, 1994

Honeycombe, Gordon, *Red Watch*, Hutchinson, 1976

Jackson, Eric W., *London's Fire Brigades*, Longmans, 1966

Wallington, Neil, *Fireman – A Personal Account*, David and Charles, 1979

Wallington, Neil, *Firemen at War*, David and Charles, 1982

Wallington, Neil, *Firefighter!* Firestorm Publications, 1992

INDEX

Special Services: (non-fire emergencies)

Fire Stations: